MORE MIND JOGGERS!

102 Ready-to-Use Activities That Make Kids *Think*

Susan S. Petreshene

Illustrated by Ron Schultz

THE CENTER FOR APPLIED
RESEARCH IN EDUCATION
West Nyack, New York 10995

© 1989 by

THE CENTER FOR APPLIED
RESEARCH IN EDUCATION

West Nyack, N.Y.

10 9 8 7 6 5 4 3 2 1

TO A VERY SPECIAL FAMILY

Library of Congress Cataloging-in-Publication Data

Petreshene, Susan S.
      More mind joggers! : 102 ready-to-use activities that make
kids think / Susan S. Petreshene : illustrated by Ron
Schultz.
        p. cm.
      ISBN 0-87628-584-1
      1. Thought and thinking—Study and teaching (Elementary)
2. Reasoning—Study and teaching (Elementary) 3.
Mathematics—Study and teaching (Elementary) 4. Language
arts—Study and teaching (Elementary) 5. Creative activities and
seat work—Handbooks, manuals, etc. I. Title
LB1590.3.P48 1988   88-25869
370.15′2—dc19   CIP

ISBN 0-87628-584-1

**THE CENTER FOR APPLIED
RESEARCH IN EDUCATION**
BUSINESS & PROFESSIONAL DIVISION
A division of Simon & Schuster
West Nyack, New York 10995

Printed in the United States of America

ABOUT THIS RESOURCE

For most teachers there are several ongoing dilemmas. "How can I fill unplanned-for extra minutes with productive activities that make kids really think?" "What do I do with students who complete assignments early or want extra challenges? I want to provide worthwhile enrichment activities for them, but..." "Where can I find some creative homework assignments that I can give to all my students?" "What type of activities can I provide for my lower ability or remedial students to help develop thinking and reasoning skills? My students would benefit so much from experiences of this type, but..."

More Mind Joggers! 102 Ready-to-Use Activities that Make Kids Think has been designed to solve just such problems with *quality* activities. Included are "Total Group Activities," "Reproducible Activity Pages," and "Individual or Partner Activities."

Total Group Activities can be used with the entire class when you have a few spare minutes before recess, lunch, a special event, or when a lesson finishes early. Here you will find a wide variety of ready-to-use activities that require *no preparation* and use simple materials like paper and pencil, chalk and chalkboard, or no materials at all.

The Reproducible Activity Pages that accompany many activities may be used either in conjunction with the Total Group Activity or independently. How you use these materials will vary from time to time, depending on what is most appropriate for your students. Sometimes you may wish to use the Total Group Activity as an introduction. The reproducible page can then be given to all students as an enrichment activity or as a homework assignment that requires them to think and reason. At other times, you will find it works well to reverse the order, having students do the reproducible page first, followed by the Total Group Activity. There may also be times when you decide to use the reproducible page without doing the Total Group Activity at all.

The reproducible pages are also effective when used with students who complete their assignments early or who want extra challenges. Since complete directions are given on each of these pages, it is not necessary for you to stop what you are doing to explain the activity. Instead, make the reproducible pages available for the students, and they can proceed on their own. Additional ideas for students who complete their assignments early can be found in the Individual or Partner Adaptations that accompany many activities.

More Mind Joggers! places at your fingertips 102 "quick" activities for grades K–6, plus 82 reproducible pages for grades 2–6. The activities and reproducible pages are divided into four major subject and skill areas: Thinking and Reasoning, Math, Language and Writing, and Listening and Remembering.

A number of the activities stimulate creative thinking, rather than have the students search for a single right answer. Many of the activities parallel standardized test items and provide practice in the specific thought patterns required by such tests. Others can be used to introduce a new concept or to review a previously taught skill. Most of the activities can serve as extensions of regular class work. Most important, *all* are meant to be productive skill-reinforcers or extenders.

Whether you are a teacher, student teacher, substitute teacher, or classroom aide, whenever you find yourself faced with unexpected free time or searching for worthwhile homework assignments or enrichment activities for students who completed their work early, you can open this resource and quickly find a ready-to-use activity. The handy Activities/Skills Index provides a convenient listing of all activities by subject matter, skill area, grade level, and group size.

For each activity, you'll find the same easy-to-use format that provides

- activity number and title
- subject and skill reinforced
- appropriate grade levels for use
- appropriate classroom groups for use
- complete list of materials needed (if any)
- step-by-step activity directions
- adaptations for other groups
- activity lists of words, questions, problems, and topics
- complete answer keys

Plus, many activities are accompanied by a reproducible page that includes

- appropriate grade levels for use
- answer key

If you keep *More Mind Joggers!* handy, you will have a wide variety of stimulating activities ready for use at a moment's notice to make those spare minutes really count. I hope you and your students enjoy them.

Susan S. Petreshene

SUGGESTIONS FOR USING THESE ACTIVITIES MOST EFFECTIVELY

More Mind Joggers! 102 Ready-to-Use Activities that Make Kids Think is a collection of 102 quick activities to develop thinking skills for students in grades K–6, plus 82 reproducible pages for grades 2–6. It presents activities that are ready to go at a moment's notice to help students spend spare time productively. The activities are also very effective when used to provide variety and enrichment for the existing curriculum.

This resource is divided into the following major skill areas:

Thinking and Reasoning Activities

Math Activities

Language and Writing Activities

Listening and Remembering Activities

Each section is divided into "Total Group Activities," "Individual or Partner Activities," and "Reproducible Activity Pages." In each of these sections, the activities are designed primarily for use with the groups designated in the boxes at the top of the page, but many provide adaptations for other groups. The Activities/Skills Index provides a simple keying system so you can select activities appropriate to specific group sizes quickly and easily.

The activities within each subsection are arranged in order from lower grade to upper grade so you can select the activity most suitable to your students' level. If the level of the Total Group Activity differs from the Individual or Partner Activity, the new level is indicated next to the heading, "Adaptation for an Individual Student (Grade X–X)." The appropriate level is found next to the heading of each reproducible page: "Reproducible Activity Page (Grade X–X)."

Total Group Activities

When using the Total Group Activities, consider using one or more of the following implementation suggestions:

1. Alternate activities from several different sections. Leave markers indicating where to resume when you return to a specific section so you won't repeat activities.

2. Select a specific activity to be used as an introduction to a new skill or as a review of previously learned concepts.

3. When writing lesson plans, familiarize yourself with several activities that you feel will benefit your students. Mark these for ready access during the week.

4. Allot a regular time period for using the activities. You will find that there will be much class interaction and involvement during the five to fifteen minutes of activity time, resulting in an enjoyable break in the routine for both you and your students. This type of break is especially

effective when it follows intensive academic studies, silent reading periods, or active periods such as recess or physical education.

Some of the Total Group Activities may be adapted for use by individual students or by partners. These uses have been coded at the top right-hand corner of the page. Necessary materials are listed (if different from those of the Total Group Activity), and adaptations are provided.

Individual or Partner Activities

These activities have been designed to fill a need different from that of the Total Group Activities. Here are productive time-fillers for students who complete their assignments early or who want extra challenges.

Each of the Individual or Partner Activities can be introduced to the entire class in a few minutes either at the beginning of the day or prior to a specific related assignment. Then, when a student unexpectedly finishes work ahead of time, you can use these activities to challenge or reinforce appropriate skills for that specific student.

Individual activities sometimes result in a puzzle, problem, or other product that can serve as a challenge for other students during their free time. For example, if one student has made a "Roving Letters" puzzle (Activity 90), his or her puzzle, directions, and clues are written on paper with the answers on the reverse side and left for others to solve. You may want to designate a box, file folder, or bulletin board space where challenges may be placed. Or, you may compile these challenges in a special puzzle book for individual or whole-class use.

Keep track of Individual or Partner Activities that have been introduced to the whole class by maintaining a posted list of these activities. By glancing at this list, both you and your students can quickly answer the question, "What can I do now?"

Reproducible Activity Pages

Reproducible pages accompany many of the activities. You may photocopy a class set or make one copy that can then be thermofaxed and duplicated.

Consider using the Reproducible Activity Pages in one of the following ways:

1. After doing a Total Group Activity, give all students the accompanying Reproducible Page as a class enrichment activity or as homework.
2. Prior to doing the Total Group Activity, give students the Reproducible Page. At a later time, use the Total Group Activity to review the material.
3. Use the Reproducible Page by itself, without doing the Total Group Activity.
4. Make Reproducible Pages available for students who complete their assignments early.

Regardless of how you decide to use the Reproducible Pages, you will know you are providing material that helps your students practice their thinking and reasoning skills while reinforcing or extending the basic curriculum.

Format Designed for Easiest Use

More Mind Joggers! has been formatted so you can quickly select appropriate activities for on-the-spot use. The Activities/Skills Index helps you find suitable activities and reproducible pages for particular groups of students in specific subject areas. The format of each activity also helps you decide at a glance whether it is best for your needs at the moment. And you can flip from one activity to another without having to refer to material elsewhere in the book. Even when directions remain the same from one activity to another, they have been repeated to make each activity a self-contained unit.

As shown in the sample activity format below, each activity begins with the subject and skill in the upper right corner of the page. The upper left corner gives the grade-level designation. At the top of the page you'll find the activity number and title, followed by a complete list of all materials needed (if any). Boxes are checked to indicate whether a reproducible page accompanies the activity and to indicate the specific groups with which the activity may be used.

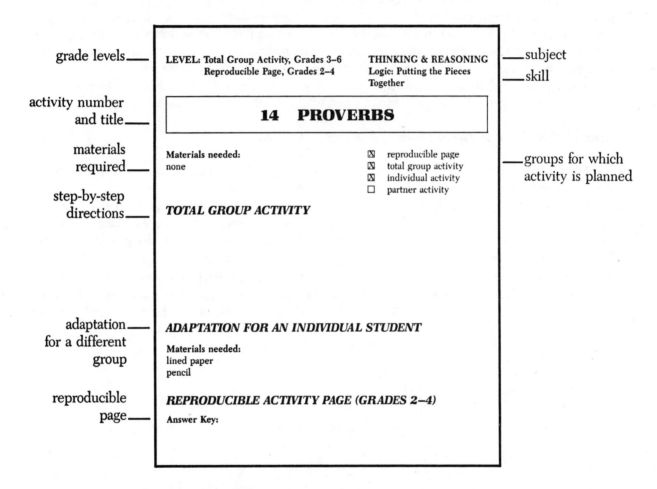

grade levels ——

activity number and title ——

materials required ——

step-by-step directions ——

adaptation for a different group ——

reproducible page ——

LEVEL: Total Group Activity, Grades 3–6
Reproducible Page, Grades 2–4

THINKING & REASONING
Logic: Putting the Pieces Together

—— subject
—— skill

14 PROVERBS

Materials needed:
none

☒ reproducible page
☒ total group activity
☒ individual activity
☐ partner activity

—— groups for which activity is planned

TOTAL GROUP ACTIVITY

ADAPTATION FOR AN INDIVIDUAL STUDENT

Materials needed:
lined paper
pencil

REPRODUCIBLE ACTIVITY PAGE (GRADES 2–4)

Answer Key:

Then each activity is clearly explained, step by step, for the primary group for which it is intended. Adaptations for other groups follow the primary use. Variations show how an activity can be altered for variety, and Follow-Up Activities extend the activity in other time slots.

If a Reproducible Activity Page accompanies the activity, it is listed next, along with the designated grade level and answer key.

Finally, lists of words, questions, problems, topics, and so on, are provided for the activity. Answer keys are supplied whenever possible, set off at the end of each activity for your convenience. In most cases, however, any answer that can be supported by good reasoning should be accepted. The supplied answers are noted as samples only.

Markers and Notes

A few well-placed markers are invaluable in getting the most from this book. These make it possible for you, or for a substitute teacher or classroom aide, to have a variety of activities marked for use at a moment's notice.

Markers are also helpful for tagging activities with lists of words, questions, problems, etc. These lists are arranged in order of difficulty, so they should be scanned to determine where to start and stop with your students. This information can then be written on a marker or directly on the page.

When you use part of a list, place a marker in the book and write a note indicating where you stopped. This will let you quickly know where to begin when you return to the activity at a later time.

You may also wish to make brief notes on the activity page regarding your students' responses and reactions. These notes will be quite useful when working with students the following year.

How to Decide Who Goes First in Partner Activities

For partner activities, it is helpful to have a quick way to determine who goes first. Suggest to students that they use either of the following methods.

Odd/Even: One student chooses "odd" and the other "even." Each student puts a hand behind his or her back and together they silently count, "1-2-3." On "3," both students thrust a hand in front of them with one to five fingers showing. If the total number of fingers is odd, the player who chose "odd" goes first. If the total is even, the other player gets the first turn.

Which Hand? One student puts both hands behind his or her back and places a small object in one hand. Both hands are then held in front of the other player, who tries to guess which hand contains the object. If correct, that player goes first. Otherwise, the person holding the object goes first.

ACTIVITIES/SKILLS INDEX

THINKING AND REASONING ACTIVITIES

ABOUT THE AUTHOR

Susan S. Petreshene, M.A. (California State University, Sonoma), has been an elementary classroom teacher for more than fifteen years in the public schools of Concord and Novato, California. She is the author of many articles in professional journals such as *Instructor* and *Social Studies Review,* and has also written three practical books for teachers, *The Complete Guide to Learning Centers* (Pendragon House, Inc., 1978); *Teaching Reading Skills: Visual, Auditory, and Kinesthetic Activities* (Zaner-Bloser, 1981), coauthored with Walter B. Barbe, Ph.D.; and *Mind Joggers! 5- to 15-Minute Activities that Make Kids Think* (The Center for Applied Research in Education, 1985).

Mrs. Petreshene is a frequent speaker at professional conferences and workshops and has served as a consultant to many school districts in the areas of individualized instruction and classroom management. She has also taught at various U.S. colleges and universities.

ACTIVITIES

1 FIND MY SECRET CATEGORY

Materials needed:

☒ reproducible page
☒ total group activity
☐ individual activity
☐ partner activity

TOTAL GROUP ACTIVITY

When brainstorming classification topics, it is fun to structure the activity so that children must stretch their minds beyond the common, more obvious categories. This activity is designed to do just that, resulting in a real challenge for students.

When working with students in grades 2–6, read the first two words from the following list and ask students to name another word that they think belongs in the same category. Explain that these are "very tricky" categories and that their first guess will probably not fit in the secret category. However, the word that *doesn't* fit will provide a clue to help them uncover how the words are grouped.

If the first guess does not belong in the category say, "No, _____ does not go with my secret category, but that was a good guess. How else might _____ and _____ (the two words you read) go together?"

After three incorrect guesses, repeat the first two words and add one of the additional hints as a further clue to the identity of the secret category.

If students continue to have difficulty discovering how the words are grouped, add the remaining additional hint, reading all four words.

When students have named five words that belong in the group, have a volunteer identify the secret category.

Variation (Grades K–1)

When working with younger students, read all four words (the two initial words *plus* the ones that provide additional hints). Although this simplifies the activity somewhat, it still provides a real challenge for younger students and gives them practice in thinking about categories that go beyond the more usual ones.

What Is the Secret Category?

1. pencil, paper (**things in the classroom**)
   additional hints: books, chalkboard

2. glass, jar (**things made of glass**)
   additional hints: light bulb, windshield

3. peach, plum (**foods that have pits or seeds that we do not eat**)
   additional hints: avocado, cherry

4. wood, bark (**things that float**)
    additional hints: cork, boat

5. signs, bumper stickers (**things that can be read**)
    additional hints: newspapers, books

6. washing machine, clothes dryer (**things that have motors**)
    additional hints: refrigerator, car

7. soup, hot chocolate (**things that are hot**)
    additional hints: volcano, fire

8. car, motorcycle (**things with wheels**)
    additional hints: shopping cart, wheelbarrow

9. snail, turtle (**things that have a shell**)
    additional hints: crab, nut

10. guinea pig, mouse (**caged pets**)
    additional hints: hamster, parrot

11. banana, orange (**foods that have a peel that you do not eat**)
    additional hints: grapefruit, pineapple

12. shoes, gloves (**things that come in pairs**)
    additional hints: socks, twins

13. crash, bang (**things that sound like what they mean**)
    additional hints: buzz, fizzle

14. ice, water vapor (**words that have to do with weather**)
    additional hints: temperature, rain

15. rose, honeysuckle (**things that have a nice smell**)
    additional hints: perfume, vanilla

REPRODUCIBLE PAGE (GRADES 3–6)

Answer Key: (1) items made of wood, (2) things that are sticky, (3) things that have handles.

FIND MY SECRET CATEGORY

Read the first group of words below. The first two words belong in my category. The third word is *not* part of the category. The fourth word *does* belong in my group of words.

Try to figure out my secret category. Write one more word that would go in the category. Then write what you think the category is.

These words belong in my category.   table, chair

This word does not belong.   couch

This word is part of my category.   ruler

Write one more word that belongs. _____

What is my secret category? _____

* * *

These words belong in my category.   jelly, honey

This word does not belong.   butter

This word is part of my category.   scotch tape

Write one more word that belongs. _____

What is my secret category? _____

* * *

These words belong in my category.   scooter, bicycle

This word does not belong.   skateboard

This word is part of my category.   pocketbook

Write one more word that belongs. _____

What is my secret category? _____

2 THROW ONE AWAY

Materials needed:

☒ reproducible page
☒ total group activity
☒ individual activity
☐ partner activity

TOTAL GROUP ACTIVITY

Read four or five words from the following list and have the students pick out the one word that doesn't fit with the others. Read the words in each group slowly the first time, then repeat them slowly. The repetition and slow pace are important because the students need to listen carefully and check the validity of their original answers. Ask students to raise their hands to give the answer *after* you have read the words twice. When answers are given, students should explain their reasoning to provide examples for those who are less secure. Any answer backed by logical reasoning should be accepted whether or not it appears in this book as the answer. If students are unable to determine the word that doesn't fit in the category, provide a clue to steer their thinking in the right direction. For example, if the words had been: grasshopper, frog, toad, snake, you might say, "Think about how each of these animals move."

This is a good activity to use when you want children to settle down after an active period.

ADAPTATION FOR AN INDIVIDUAL STUDENT (GRADES 3–6)

Materials needed:

lined paper (6″ × 9″ for class book)
pencil

The student lists four words on a piece of paper, three of which go together in some logical way. One of the words should not fit with the others, but should have some common elements. Explain that if the mismatched word is too different, there will be no challenge in solving the puzzle.

The answer and its explanation should be written on the reverse side of the paper. For example: (front side) dog, gopher, cat, guinea pig; (reverse side) gopher. It is not a pet.

When a number of these papers have been collected, they can be assembled into an interesting and stimulating class book to be used individually or as a total group activity.

Which One Doesn't Match?

1. parakeet, kitten, calf, guinea pig (**calf—not a household pet**)
2. peach, apple, potato, orange (**potato—not a fruit**)
3. gorilla, tiger, dog, zebra (**dog—not a zoo animal**)

4. saw, pliers, wood, wrench (**wood—not a tool**)

5. crayons, felt pens, paper, colored chalk (**paper—not an implement used for drawing**)

6. duck, goose, rooster, parrot (**parrot—not a farm animal**)

7. large, enormous, size, huge (**size—not a word that means "big"**)

8. house, table, dresser, chair (**house—not a piece of furniture**)

9. feet, claws, cat, beak (**cat—not part of a bird**)

10. stand, jump, spin, leap (**stand—not a movement**)

11. puppy, dog, calf, fawn (**dog—not a baby animal**)

12. root beer, lemonade, ice cream, milk (**ice cream—not a drink**)

13. truck, airplane, car, bus (**airplane—not a vehicle that is used for traveling on the ground**)

14. pencil, paper, workbook, chalkboard (**pencil—not something to write on**)

15. grasshopper, frog, toad, snake (**snake—not an animal that jumps**)

16. parrot, sparrow, parakeet, canary (**sparrow—not a pet bird**)

17. checkers, chess, tic-tac-toe, bingo (**tic-tac-toe—not a board game**)

18. carpenter, nails, hammer, wood (**carpenter—not an object used by a carpenter**)

19. bat, glove, ball, player (**player—not an object used for baseball**)

20. milk, egg, cottage cheese, yogurt (**egg—not a dairy product**)

21. washing machine, soap, dryer, dishwasher (**soap—not a household appliance**)

22. boots, raincoat, rain, umbrella (**rain—not something used in rainy weather**)

23. ruler, yardstick, foot, measuring tape (**foot—not a tool for measurement**)

24. mad, punishment, angry, furious (**punishment—not a word that means "angry"**)

25. basketball, tennis, badminton, racquetball (**basketball—not a game that uses a racquet**)

26. mud, dirty, filthy, soiled (**mud—not a word that means "dirty"**)

27. fly, spider, beetle, termite (**spider—not an insect**)

28. geranium, vine, daffodil, violet (**vine—not a flower**)

29. trumpet, flute, trombone, tuba (**flute—not a brass instrument**)

30. squash, apple, fig, date (**squash—not a fruit**)

31. rain, hail, sleet, snow (**rain—not a form of frozen precipitation**)

32. crocodile, turtle, toad, lizard (**toad—not a reptile**)

33. amusing, entertaining, exciting, humorous (**exciting—not a word that means "funny"**)

34. acorn, almond, pecan, prune (**prune—not a nut**)

35. whale, walrus, shark, seal (**shark—not a mammal**)

36. runway, wharf, hangar, control tower (**wharf—not related to aviation**)

37. Boston, Massachusetts, Texas, Florida (**Boston—not a state**)

38. fatigued, rambunctious, weary, tired (**rambunctious—not a word that means "tired"**)

39. sage, spinach, parsley, mint (**spinach—not an herb**)

40. island, peninsula, bay, ocean (**ocean—not a land form**)

41. deliberately, speedily, rapidly, hastily (**deliberately—not a word that means "quickly"**)

42. star, space, planet, meteor (**space—not a celestial body**)

43. elm, oak, geranium, maple (**geranium—not a tree**)
44. cactus, fern, sidewinder, sand (**fern—not part of a desert environment**)
45. risky, adventure, hazardous, unsafe (**adventure—not a word that means "unsafe"**)
46. gold, silver, diamond, platinum (**diamond—not a metal**)
47. venison, veal, cattle, pork (**cattle—not a type of meat**)
48. peso, gold, dollar, franc (**gold—not a form of currency**)
49. Africa, Antarctica, United States, Australia (**United States—not a continent**)
50. rain gauge, barometer, thermometer, compass (**compass—not a weather instrument**)

REPRODUCIBLE ACTIVITY PAGE (GRADES 2–3)

Answer Key: (1) dirt—not part of a flower, (2) parrot—not a farm animal, (3) house—not a piece of furniture, (4) fur—not part of a bird, (5) dog—not a baby animal, (6) wood—not a tool, (7) milk—not a dessert.

NAME _____

THROW ONE AWAY

Read the words below. Find the one word that doesn't fit with the others and write it in the box. Then use the words in the *WORD BANK* to help you tell why the word you wrote doesn't go with the others.

WORD BANK		
furniture	baby	farm
piece	animal	bird
part	dessert	tool

WHICH WORD DOESN'T MATCH?

1. petal, stem, flower, dirt

   [dirt]

   Why? _not part of a flower_

2. duck, goose, hen, parrot

   [ ]

   Why? _____

3. bed, table, chair, house

   [ ]

   Why? _____

4. fur, wing, claws, beak

   [ ]

   Why? _____

5. puppy, dog, fawn, kitten

   [ ]

   Why? _____

6. saw, drill, hammer, wood

   [ ]

   Why? _____

7. ice cream, milk, cake, cookie

   [ ]

   Why? _____

3   A TYPE OF...

Materials needed:

TOTAL GROUP ACTIVITY

Name an object from the following list and have the students tell you what category it belongs in. For example: "Checkers is a type of..." (game); "Daisy is a type of..." (flower).

Encourage students to be as specific as possible when naming categories. (This will vary according to the age and ability level of your students.) If "daisy" is identified as a kind of plant, acknowledge the answer, but ask if the student can give a word that describes the category more precisely. Possible answers have been listed below. However, in many cases there will be more than one correct response. Accept all responses that seem appropriate.

This Is a Type of...

1. potato is a type of (**vegetable**)
2. dresser is a type of (**furniture**)
3. giraffe is a type of (**wild animal**)
4. coat is a type of (**clothing**)
5. hopscotch is a type of (**game**)
6. doll is a type of (**toy**)
7. parakeet is a type of (**bird**)
8. green is a type of (**color**)
9. wrench is a type of (**tool**)
10. rose is a type of (**flower**)
11. cat is a type of (**pet**)
12. goat is a type of (**farm animal**)
13. baseball is a type of (**sport**)
14. orange juice is a type of (**drink**)
15. snow is a type of (**weather**)
16. pudding is a type of (**dessert**)
17. moth is a type of (**insect**)
18. cold cereal is a type of (**breakfast food**)
19. boa constrictor is a type of (**snake**)
20. rocking is a type of (**movement**)
21. centimeter is a type of (**measurement**)
22. salmon is a type of (**fish**)
23. cottage is a type of (**house/building**)
24. quail is a type of (**bird**)
25. kayak is a type of (**boat**)
26. cub is a type of (**baby animal**)
27. redwood is a type of (**tree**)
28. quarter is a type of (**coin**)
29. collie is a type of (**dog**)
30. ferry is a type of (**transportation/boat**)
31. yogurt is a type of (**dairy product**)
32. magazine is a type of (**reading material**)
33. squid is a type of (**sea animal**)
34. flute is a type of (**instrument**)
35. orchid is a type of (**flower**)
36. ruby is a type of (**jewel/precious stone**)
37. being excited is a type of (**emotion**)
38. pen is a type of (**writing instrument**)
39. sickle is a type of (**tool**)
40. chartreuse is a type of (**color**)

41. rifle is a type of (**weapon**)
42. lizard is a type of (**reptile**)
43. silver is a type of (**precious metal**)
44. pomegranate is a type of (**fruit**)
45. newt is a type of (**amphibian**)
46. macaroni is a type of (**pasta**)
47. polo is a type of (**sport**)

48. baler is a type of (**farm equipment**)
49. veal is a type of (**meat**)
50. granite is a type of (**rock**)
51. carbon dioxide is a type of (**gas**)
52. timpani is a type of (**instrument**)
53. spaghetti is a type of (**pasta**)
54. plateau is a type of (**geological feature**)

REPRODUCIBLE ACTIVITY PAGE (GRADES 2–3)

Answer Key: (1) weather, (2) baby animal, (3) color, (4) coin, (5) reptile, (6) metal, (7) tool, (8) sea animal, (9) flower, (10) farm animal, (11) insect, (12) building, (13) bird, (14) game.

Suggestion: If you do not have time to duplicate the reproducible page, as an alternate procedure have the student make a list of as many objects as he or she can think of and indicate the category or categories in which each belongs.

A TYPE OF...

A cat is a type of pet. Baseball is a type of sport.

Find a word in the *WORD BANK* that tells about each of the words below.

WORD BANK

baby animal	coin	game
weather	metal	reptile
color	sea animal	bird
flower	farm animal	tool
insect		building

---

1. Snow is a type of
   weather .

2. A fawn is a type of
   _____ .

3. Gray is a type of
   _____ .

4. A dime is a type of
   _____ .

5. Snakes are a type of
   _____ .

6. Brass is a type of
   _____ .

7. Hammers are a type of
   _____ .

8. A squid is a type of
   _____ .

9. Tulips are a type of
   _____ .

10. A goat is a type of
    _____ .

11. Moths are a type of
    _____ .

12. A barn is a type of
    _____ .

13. Parrots are a type of
    _____ .

14. Hopscotch is a type of
    _____ .

Now make one of your own.

_____ is a type of _____ .

4   JOBS DEPEND ON JOBS

Materials needed:

☒ reproducible page
☒ total group activity
☐ individual activity
☐ partner activity

TOTAL GROUP ACTIVITY

This activity helps students understand what various jobs entail and the interrelationship between jobs. As the activity progresses, it is important to ask questions so that students are encouraged to think beyond their initial, more obvious responses.

To begin the activity, select one of the following occupations that is familiar to your students. Ask the students to define what the person does. Then have them think of other jobs that need to be done in order for *this person* to do his or her job. Also have them identify other related jobs that affect the quality of the goods or services delivered. For instance a commercial airline pilot relies on the ground crew to check the mechanics and to fuel the plane, and the air traffic controller to oversee the safety of the plane's takeoff and landing. Related jobs include the reservation clerk to book flights and sell tickets, the cooks to prepare the food, a crew to clean the inside of the plane, flight attendants, etc.

You'll find students involved in considerable thinking and discussion throughout this activity.

Occupations

1.   radio or television announcer
2.   hotel waiter or waitress
3.   movie theater manager
4.   contractor
5.   heavy equipment operator
6.   electricity or gas meter reader
7.   switchboard operator
8.   proofreader
9.   layout artist
10.   sales representative
11.   camera technician for films or TV
12.   draftman
13.   computer programmer (**writes instructions that "tell" the computer exactly what to do**)
14.   surveyor (**makes measurements to determine boundaries of property, measurements for map making, and measurements for use in the construction of roads, buildings, bridges, etc.**)

15. ophthalmologist (doctor who examines eyes, treats diseases of the eyes, and performs eye-related surgery)

16. civil engineer (designs and oversees the construction of structures, designs water supply and sewage systems, transportation systems, and assists with city planning)

REPRODUCIBLE ACTIVITY PAGE (GRADES 3–6)

If this activity is used with the entire class, distribute the reproducible page and briefly discuss its format. After students have had time to complete the page, have them share their answers. Discuss the diversity of their thinking and have them share additional ideas that occur to them as they listen to the thoughts of others.

Answer Key: Answers will vary, but representative answers follow. All answers that can be backed by logical reasoning should be accepted. (1) *grocery store checker:* stock clerk, butcher, produce person, store manager, maintenance person, someone to keep the store clean, bookkeeper, farmer, manufacturers, delivery people... (2) *newspaper reporter:* printer, photographer, people to determine the layout of the paper, people to run the presses, editors, managers, telephone operators, people to take subscription orders, collection agents, advertising staff... (3) *florist:* people to arrange flowers, person to take orders, bookkeeper, delivery person, person to clean store, manufacturers of needed supplies (cards, wire, ribbon, containers, etc.), people who market and sell the supplies, flower growers...

Suggestion: If you do not have time to duplicate the reproducible page, as an alternate procedure assign several occupations and have students list: (1) jobs that need to be done in order for the person to do his or her job, (2) related jobs that affect the quality of the goods or services delivered.

JOBS DEPEND ON JOBS

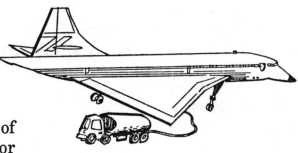

Look at the three jobs listed below. Think of other jobs that need to be done in order for each of these people to do *their jobs*. Also think of jobs that affect the quality of the goods or services delivered. For instance, a commercial airline pilot needs the ground crew to check the mechanics and to fuel the plane, and the air traffic controller to oversee the safety of the plane's takeoff and landing. Related jobs include the reservation clerk to book flights and sell tickets, the cooks to prepare the food, a crew to clean the inside of the plane, flight attendants, etc.

WHAT OTHER JOBS ARE IMPORTANT TO EACH OF THESE PEOPLE?

GROCERY STORE CHECKER	NEWSPAPER REPORTER	FLORIST
_____	_____	_____
_____	_____	_____
_____	_____	_____
_____	_____	_____
_____	_____	_____
_____	_____	_____
_____	_____	_____
_____	_____	_____
_____	_____	_____
_____	_____	_____

5 LIBRARY SEARCH

Materials needed:

☒ reproducible page
☒ total group activity
☐ individual activity
☐ partner activity

TOTAL GROUP ACTIVITY

Before beginning this activity, remind students that the library is divided into two major sections: nonfiction (fact) and fiction. Discuss the kinds of books found in each section. Make certain that students understand that nonfiction books are grouped by category. Thus, all the books about animals are together and subdivided by specific groups: insects, reptiles, birds, etc.

As you name each topic below, ask students to tell whether the book would be found in the fiction or nonfiction section of the library. If the book is nonfiction, have them explain what other books would be grouped with it. For instance, books about hummingbirds would be grouped with other books about birds.

What Books Would You Find Grouped With This Type of Book?

Note: The answers given below are intended as a general guideline, as the extent of a library collection will often make a difference in how books are arranged.

1. baseball (**sports**)
2. ants (**animals, insects**)
3. tall tales (**fairy tales, fables, legends**)
4. making puppets (**painting, crafts, hobbies**)
5. snakes (**animals, reptiles**)
6. jokes (**jokes, riddles, puzzles**)
7. drawing (**painting, crafts**)
8. Alaska (**geography, history, travel**)
9. ostrich (**animals, birds**)
10. skiing (**recreational sports, boating, hang gliding**)
11. stars (**astronomy, planets, constellations**)
12. coin collecting (**hobbies, collecting**)
13. Vikings (**geography, history, travel**)
14. whales (**animals, mammals**)
15. electricity (**science, gases, fluids, heat**)

16. Benjamin Franklin (biographies or history)
17. Mother Goose rhymes (fairy tales, tall tales, fables)
18. knitting (crafts, handiwork, hobbies)
19. flowers–(plants)
20. star quarterbacks (sports or biographies)
21. Daniel Boone (biographies or history)
22. riddles (jokes, riddles, puzzles)
23. bees (animals, insects)
24. candle making (crafts, hobbies)
25. Russia (geography, history, travel)
26. Joe Namath (biographies or sports)
27. Mars (astronomy, planets, stars)
28. King Arthur legends (fairy tales, folk tales)
29. photography (art, photography)
30. soccer (sports)
31. tiger (animals, mammals)
32. funny poems (other poems and plays)
33. microscopes (science)
34. Antarctica (geography, history, travel)
35. Albert Einstein (biographies or science)
36. pelican (animals, birds)
37. the sun (astronomy, planets, stars)
38. Wilma Rudolph (biographies or sports)
39. puzzles (puzzles, jokes, riddles)
40. octopus (animals, sea animals)
41. Olympic games (sports)
42. Brothers Grimm fairy tales (folk tales, legends)
43. horseback riding (recreational sports, boating, skiing)
44. stamp collecting (hobbies, collections)
45. butterflies (animals, insects)
46. Jupiter (astronomy, planets, stars)
47. Yellowstone (geography, history, travel)
48. sound waves (science, gases, fluids, heat)
49. panda (animals, mammals)
50. trees (plants)
51. Florence Nightingale (biographies or history)
52. constellations (astronomy, planets, stars)
53. Aesop fables (fairy tales, folk tales, legends)
54. turtles (animals, reptiles)

55. limericks (**riddles, rhymes**)
56. falcon (**animals, birds**)
57. Alexander Graham Bell (**biographies or science**)
58. Gold Rush (**history, geography, travel**)
59. wild flowers (**plants**)
60. hang gliding (**recreational sports, boating, skiing**)

REPRODUCIBLE ACTIVITY PAGE (GRADES 3–5)

Answer Key: (Answers for "Major Sections" follow. Other books that students list will vary. Accept all logical answers.) (1) sports, (2) astronomy, (3) tales, (4) hobbies/collections, (5) animals, (6) recreational sports, (7) hobbies/collections, (8) sports.

LIBRARY SEARCH

Libraries are divided into two major sections: *fiction* (pretend stories) and *nonfiction* (factual books). Fiction books are put on the shelves in alphabetical order, according to the author's last name. Nonfiction books are grouped by category. Therefore, all the books about animals are together. Then these are subdivided by specific groups: insects, reptiles, birds, etc.

Listed below are some of the nonfiction sections in libraries.

SPORTS	ANIMALS	ASTRONOMY	RECREATIONAL SPORTS	HOBBIES/ COLLECTIONS	TALES

Read each book topic in the chart below. Write the name of the major section where books of this type would be found. Then write two kinds of books that you think would be grouped with it. For instance, the major section for a book about hummingbirds would be animals and it would be placed on the shelf with other books about birds. Nearby would be books about mammals, insects, etc.

Since the number of books in a library makes a slight difference in how books are arranged, you may want to go to your own library to check your answers.

BOOK TOPIC	MAJOR SECTION	OTHER BOOKS THAT WOULD BE GROUPED NEAR THIS BOOK
1. lacrosse	sports	hockey, football
2. Saturn		
3. fables		
4. knitting		
5. whales		
6. horseback riding		
7. candle making		
8. baseball		

6   DOMESTICATED/WILD ANIMALS

Materials needed:

☒ reproducible page
☒ total group activity
☒ individual activity
☐ partner activity

TOTAL GROUP ACTIVITY

Explain to students that domesticated animals are animals that once were wild, but have been tamed and trained to live with people or to be of use to them. Give the example of turkeys which were once wild birds, but now are raised on farms as a source of food. Although some turkeys remain in the wild, the majority of turkeys today are domesticated. Therefore, for this activity, turkeys are listed as a domesticated animal.

Read the name of each animal from the following list and have students wiggle their fingers in front of them if the animal is wild. If the majority of that type of animal is domesticated, they should clasp their hands together. Remind them to think before responding. To provide them thinking time, after you read the word hold up your open hand and silently count to five. They should indicate their answers when you close your fist.

Variation

Students may respond by standing up for wild animals and remaining seated for domesticated animals.

ADAPTATION FOR AN INDIVIDUAL STUDENT (GRADES 2–3)

Materials needed:

lined paper
pencil

Have the student draw a line down the middle of a piece of paper and label the two sections "Domesticated" and "Wild." In the appropriate column, the student should list as many animals as possible for each category.

Is It Wild or Domesticated?

1. zebra (**wild**)
2. turkey (**domesticated**)
3. giraffe (**wild**)

4. sheep (**domesticated**)
5. alligator (**wild**)
6. elephant (**wild**)

7. hen (**domesticated**)
8. bear (**wild**)
9. pony (**domesticated**)
10. panda (**wild**)
11. gorilla (**wild**)
12. cat (**domesticated**)
13. kangaroo (**wild**)
14. pig (**domesticated**)
15. lion (**wild**)
16. cow (**domesticated**)
17. monkey (**wild**)
18. dog (**domesticated**)
19. rooster (**domesticated**)
20. hippopotamus (**wild**)
21. boa constrictor (**wild**)
22. baboon (**wild**)
23. steer (**domesticated**)
24. leopard (**wild**)
25. anteater (**wild**)
26. donkey (**domesticated**)
27. orangutan (**wild**)
28. crocodile (**wild**)
29. mule (**domesticated**)
30. python (**wild**)
31. rhinoceros (**wild**)
32. chimpanzee (**wild**)
33. horse (**domesticated**)
34. tiger (**wild**)
35. moose (**wild**)
36. ox (**domesticated**)

REPRODUCIBLE ACTIVITY PAGE (GRADES 1–2)

Make certain students understand the definition of domesticated animal, as given in the Total Group Activity.

Answer Key: bear—wild; turkey—domesticated; cat—domesticated; monkey—wild; eagle—wild; lion—wild; cow—domesticated; pig—domesticated; tiger—wild; horse—domesticated; moose—wild.

Follow-Up Activity

Have students look at their reproducible activity page and locate (1) the domesticated animals that can also be found in the wild (turkey, pig, horse); (2) the wild animals that are *sometimes* tamed or trained (bear, monkey, lion, tiger).

NAME _____

IS THE ANIMAL WILD OR DOMESTICATED?

Read the words below. Think about each animal.

If the animal is wild, draw a line from the name of the animal to the dot under WILD.

If the animal is domesticated, draw a line from the name of the animal to the dot under DOMESTICATED.

WILD	ANIMALS	DOMESTICATED
•	hen———————————	•
•	bear	•
•	turkey	•
•	cat	•
•	monkey	•
•	eagle	•
•	lion	•
•	cow	•
•	pig	•
•	tiger	•
•	horse	•
•	moose	•

Write the name of one more wild animal in the box.

Write the name of one more domesticated animal in the box.

WILD

DOMESTICATED

7   PERSON/PLACE/OBJECT

Materials needed:
chalk
chalkboard

☒ reproducible page
☒ total group activity
☒ individual activity
☐ partner activity

TOTAL GROUP ACTIVITY

Tell students you will read the following list of words which name persons, places, or objects. Have them hold up one finger if the word names a person, two fingers if it names a place, or three fingers if it names an object.

Write the following on the chalkboard as a visual reminder:

1. person
2. place
3. object

Variation

Students may respond by standing/sitting/sitting with hands outstretched, or with tumbs up/ thumbs down/thumbs pointed outward. As a visual reminder, write the names of the categories on the chalkboard and accompany each with a stick figure illustrating the response. An alternate method is to name only one of the categories and have students listen for words that belong in the designated category. They respond by standing, putting thumbs up, or raising their arms.

Remind them to think before answering. To provide them thinking time, after you read the word hold up your opened hand and silently count to five. They should respond when you close your fist.

ADAPTATION FOR AN INDIVIDUAL STUDENT (GRADES 2–4)

Materials needed:
lined paper
pencil

The student draws two lines down a piece of paper, dividing it into three columns. The sections should be labeled "Person," "Place," and "Object." As many items as the student can think of should be listed in each of the appropriate columns.

Is It a Person, Place, or Object?

1. pilot (**person**)
2. museum (**place**)
3. reporter (**person**)
4. table (**object**)
5. bus stop (**place**)
6. restaurant (**place**)
7. mechanic (**person**)
8. lunch pail (**object**)
9. jacket (**object**)
10. sister (**person**)
11. moon (**place**)
12. school (**place**)
13. pencil (**object**)
14. aunt (**person**)
15. shell (**object**)
16. library (**place**)
17. airport (**place**)
18. physician (**person**)
19. computer (**object**)
20. church (**place**)
21. grandfather (**person**)
22. store (**place**)
23. desk (**object**)
24. flower (**object**)
25. electrician (**person**)
26. brother (**person**)
27. movie theater (**place**)
28. television (**object**)
29. carpenter (**person**)
30. ball (**object**)
31. horse (**object**)
32. ball park (**place**)
33. uncle (**person**)
34. zoo (**place**)
35. chair (**object**)
36. lawyer (**person**)
37. board game (**object**)
38. pediatrician (**person**)
39. cafeteria (**place**)
40. cousin (**person**)
41. stadium (**place**)
42. ranger (**person**)
43. vase (**object**)
44. concert hall (**place**)

REPRODUCIBLE ACTIVITY PAGE (GRADES 1–2)

Answer Key: PERSON—father, baby, mother, sister, boy, girl; PLACE—store, school, bus stop, bedroom, zoo, cave; OBJECT—sock, book, bus, coat, ball, desk.

IS IT A PERSON, PLACE, OR OBJECT?

Read each word below.

If the word is a person, write it under PERSON.
If the word is a place, write it under PLACE.
If the word is an object, write it under OBJECT.

store	bus	sister
sock	coat	zoo
father	bus stop	cave
school	mother	boy
book	bedroom	girl
baby	ball	desk

PERSON	PLACE	OBJECT
	store	

8   LAND/WATER/BOTH

Materials needed:

☒ reproducible page
☒ total group activity
☒ individual activity
☐ partner activity

TOTAL GROUP ACTIVITY

Tell students they are to determine whether the words you read from the following list name something that would be most often found on land, in water, or both on land and in water. If it is found on land, have them put both arms up in the air, like trees. If it is found in water, they should imitate a wave with one hand. For "both" they should clasp their hands together. Students who are uncertain should fold their arms.

Remind them to think before responding. To provide them thinking time, after you read the word hold up your opened hand and silently count to five. They should indicate their answer when you close your fist.

Variation

Students may respond by putting thumbs up/thumbs down/clasping hands, or by standing/sitting/clasping hands. An alternate method is to write the categories on the chalkboard and number them 1, 2, 3. Students indicate their choice by holding up the corresponding number of fingers. Or you may name only one of the categories and have students listen for words that belong in the designated category. They respond by standing, putting thumbs up, or raising their arms.

ADAPTATION FOR AN INDIVIDUAL STUDENT (GRADES 2–4)

Materials needed:

lined paper
pencil

The student draws two lines down a piece of paper, dividing it into three columns. The sections are labeled "Land," "Water," and "Both." In the appropriate column, the student lists as many items as possible for each of the categories.

Is It Found on Land, in the Water, or Both?

1. horse (**land**)
2. whale (**water**)
3. tadpole (**water**)
4. seashell (**both**)

26

  5. cat **(land)**
  6. sand **(both)**
  7. octopus **(water)**
  8. sheep **(land)**
  9. dolphin **(water)**
 10. rock **(both)**
 11. billy goat **(land)**
 12. snake **(both)**
 13. turtle **(both)**
 14. seaweed **(both)**
 15. camel **(land)**
 16. shark **(water)**
 17. frog **(both)**
 18. trout **(water)**
 19. chicken **(land)**
 20. duck **(both)**
 21. alligator **(both)**
 22. grasshopper **(land)**
 23. lobster **(water)**
 24. shrimp **(water)**
 25. turkey **(land)**
 26. snail **(both)**
 27. crab **(both)**
 28. giant squid **(water)**
 29. tarantula **(land)**
 30. seal **(both)**
 31. scallop **(water)**
 32. chimpanzee **(land)**
 33. piranha **(water)**
 34. otter **(both)**
 35. muskrat **(both)**
 36. lion **(land)**
 37. crayfish **(both)**
 38. sea urchin **(water)**
 39. giraffe **(land)**
 40. beaver **(both)**
 41. kelp **(water)**
 42. coral **(water)**
 43. horned toad **(land)**
 44. stingray **(water)**
 45. sea horse **(water)**
 46. scorpion **(land)**
 47. goose **(both)**
 48. plankton **(water)**
 49. chameleon **(land)**
 50. sand dollar **(both)**

REPRODUCIBLE ACTIVITY PAGE (GRADES 1–3)

Answer Key: (1) B, (2) L, (3) B, (4) W, (5) L, (6) B, (7) B, (8) B, (9) B, (10) L, (11) B, (12) B, (13) L, (14) L, (15) L, (16) L, (17) L, (18) B, (19) L, (20) B, (21) B, (22) W, (23) W, (24) L.

IS IT FOUND ON LAND, IN WATER, OR BOTH?

Read the words below. Think about where you would find each thing.

Write "W" if you would find it in water.
Write "L" if you would find it on land.
Write "B" if it could be found on both land and water.

1. duck _____

2. turkey _____

3. sand _____

4. shark _____

5. sheep _____

6. rock _____

7. seashell _____

8. frog _____

9. snail _____

10. grasshopper _____

11. crab _____

12. seal _____

13. lion _____

14. spider _____

15. monkey _____

16. hen _____

17. goat _____

18. goose _____

19. kitten _____

20. otter _____

21. leaf _____

22. octopus _____

23. tadpole _____

24. fox _____

©1989 by The Center for Applied Research in Education

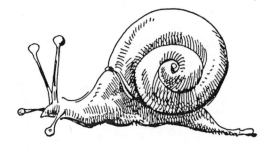

9   MALE/FEMALE/EITHER

Materials needed:

chalk
chalkboard

☒ reproducible page
☒ total group activity
☐ individual activity
☐ partner activity

TOTAL GROUP ACTIVITY

Tell students you will name an animal or person, and ask them to identify whether it is male, female, or either. You can use the example of *father* for male, *mother* for female, and *child* as a word that is used for either male or female.

Students should use the following hand signals to indicate categories.

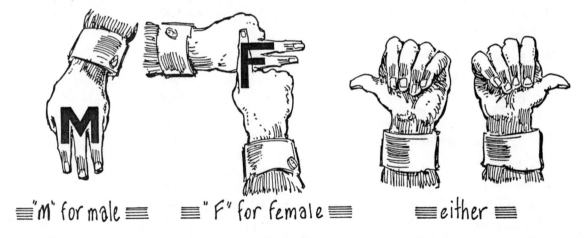

="m" for male=   ="F" for female=   =either=

Read a word, then say aloud, "One... two... three... Show me." On the signal, "Show me," students should give a hand signal to indicate the category. If they look around to see what others have done before giving their own hand signal, change the directions to "Close eyes." (Pause) "Show me... Open eyes."

As a visual reminder write the categories on the board, indicating the appropriate response for each.

Variation

Students may respond by standing/sitting/sitting with hands outstretched, or with thumbs up/thumbs down/thumbs pointed outward. An alternate method is to write the categories on the chalkboard and number them 1, 2, 3. Students indicate their choice by holding up the corresponding number of fingers. Or you may name only one of the categories. Students listen for words in the designated category and respond by standing, putting thumbs up, or raising their arms.

Do These Words Name a Male, a Female, or Both?

1. brother (**male**)
2. princess (**female**)
3. hen (**female**)
4. father (**male**)
5. child (**either**)
6. wife (**female**)
7. uncle (**male**)
8. puppy (**either**)
9. artist (**either**)
10. sister (**female**)
11. rooster (**male**)
12. waitress (**female**)
13. cow (**female**)
14. nephew (**male**)
15. daughter (**female**)
16. grandparent (**either**)
17. chicken (**either**)
18. prince (**male**)
19. parent (**either**)
20. ballerina (**female**)
21. doctor (**either**)
22. niece (**female**)
23. nurse (**either**)
24. doe (**female**)
25. pig (**either**)
26. actor (**male**)
27. cousin (**either**)
28. waiter (**male**)
29. telephone operator (**either**)
30. actress (**female**)
31. billy goat (**male**)
32. bull (**male**)
33. tadpole (**either**)
34. lioness (**female**)
35. scientist (**either**)
36. gosling (**either**)
37. boar (**male**)
38. author (**either**)
39. cub (**either**)
40. mare (**female**)
41. surgeon (**either**)
42. lamb (**either**)
43. sow (**female**)
44. buck (**male**)
45. fawn (**either**)
46. engineer (**either**)
47. stallion (**male**)
48. duckling (**either**)
49. ewe (**female**)
50. gander (**male**)
51. newscaster (**either**)
52. ram (**male**)
53. drone (**male**)
54. calf (**either**)
55. drake (**male**)

REPRODUCIBLE ACTIVITY PAGE (GRADES 3–6)

Answer Key: Answers will vary.

Suggestion: If you do not have time to duplicate the reproducible page, as an alternate procedure have students draw two lines down a piece of paper, dividing it into three columns. The sections should be labeled "Male," "Female," and "Either." As many words as they can think of for each category should be listed in the appropriate columns.

DO THESE WORDS NAME A MALE, A FEMALE, OR EITHER ONE?

Some words in the English language are used to name males (king or brother). Other words name females (sister, hen). Still other words can be used to name *either* males or females (scientist, duck).

Think of words that name people or animals. Use these to fill in as many spaces as you can in the chart below.

MALE	FEMALE	EITHER
uncle	hen	explorer

10 CITIES/COUNTRIES

Materials needed:

☒ reproducible page
☒ total group activity
☒ individual activity
☐ partner activity

TOTAL GROUP ACTIVITY

Explain to students that you will read a list of cities and countries. If you say the name of a city, they should put their thumbs up. If you name a country, they should point their thumbs down. Students who are uncertain should fold their arms. Places that are unfamiliar to students may be located on a map and briefly discussed, or you may ask for volunteers to find where the unfamiliar places are located and share the information with the class at a later time.

Remind them to think before responding. To provide ample thinking time, after you read a word hold up your opened hand and silently count to five. They should respond when you close your fist. If students look around to see what others have done before giving their own hand signal, change the directions to, "Close eyes." (Pause) "Show me.... Open Eyes."

ADAPTATION FOR AN INDIVIDUAL STUDENT (GRADES 4–6)

Materials needed:

lined paper
pencil

Have students draw a line down the middle of a piece of paper and label the two sections "Cities" and "Countries." In the appropriate column, they should list as many words as possible for each category.

Is This a City or a Country?

1. Canada (**country**)
2. Boston (**city**)
3. France (**country**)
4. London (**city**)
5. Moscow (**city**)
6. Japan (**country**)
7. Paris (**city**)
8. Italy (**country**)
9. Mexico (**country**)
10. Rome (**city**)
11. Soviet Union (**country**)
12. Chicago (**city**)
13. Australia (**country**)
14. Leningrad (**city**)
15. Germany (**country**)
16. India (**country**)
17. Rio de Janeiro (**city**)
18. Spain (**country**)

19. Iran (**country**)
20. Tokyo (**city**)
21. China (**country**)
22. Athens (**city**)
23. England (**country**)
24. Houston (**city**)
25. Switzerland (**country**)
26. Peru (**country**)
27. Shanghai (**city**)
28. Greece (**country**)
29. Ethiopia (**country**)
30. Montreal (**city**)
31. Holland (**country**)
32. Bangkok (**city**)
33. Israel (**country**)
34. Vancouver (**city**)
35. Czechoslovakia (**country**)
36. Jerusalem (**city**)
37. Guatemala (**country**)
38. Johannesburg (**city**)
39. Budapest (**city**)
40. Equador (**country**)
41. Amsterdam (**city**)
42. Denmark (**country**)
43. Hungary (**country**)
44. Sydney (**city**)
45. Turkey (**country**)
46. Vienna (**city**)
47. Brussels (**city**)
48. Sweden (**country**)
49. New Orleans (**city**)
50. Poland (**country**)
51. Stockholm (**city**)
52. Norway (**country**)
53. Libya (**country**)
54. Warsaw (**city**)
55. New Zealand (**country**)
56. Honolulu (**city**)

REPRODUCIBLE ACTIVITY PAGE (GRADES 4–6)

This page provides practice in using an atlas to determine the countries in which well-known cities are located.

Answer Key: (1) Canada, Montreal, Ottawa; (2) India, New Delhi, Bombay; (3) England, London, Plymouth; (4) China, Shanghai, Beijing; (5) Germany, Berlin, Bonn; (6) Soviet Union, Moscow, Leningrad; (7) Japan, Tokyo, Hiroshima; (8) Italy, Rome, Naples; (9) Spain, Madrid, Barcelona.

CITIES AND COUNTRIES

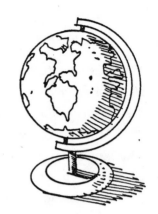

Well-known cities are listed in the box below.
Countries are listed in the chart that follows.

Match each city with the country where it is
located. If you are not certain of the location
of a city, look up the information in an atlas.

CITIES		
Bonn	London	Moscow
Tokyo	Beijing	Naples
Montreal	Hiroshima	New Delhi
Leningrad	Rome	Madrid
Barcelona	Bombay	Berlin
Shanghai	Plymouth	Ottawa

WHICH CITIES ARE FOUND IN EACH OF THE FOLLOWING COUNTRIES?

COUNTRIES	CITIES	
1. Canada		
2. India		
3. England		
4. China		
5. Germany		
6. Soviet Union		
7. Japan		
8. Italy		
9. Spain		

©1989 by The Center for Applied Research in Education

11 HOW MANY ANSWERS CAN YOU FIND?

Materials needed:

☒ reproducible page
☒ total group activity
☒ individual activity
☐ partner activity

TOTAL GROUP ACTIVITY

Read each of the following questions and have students think of as many logical answers as possible. Make certain they understand that there is *no* one right answer to any of the questions.

ADAPTATION FOR AN INDIVIDUAL STUDENT (GRADES 5–6)

Have students write as many questions as they can think of that have multiple answers. These can be used at a later time as a challenge for the total class.

Questions for Brainstorming

1. In what ways are jello and ice cream alike? (**both desserts, sweet, will melt...**) How are they different? (**One is a dairy product and the other isn't. Ice cream must be kept in the freezer but jello is kept in the refrigerator. Their textures are different.**)

2. Mrs. Kelly looked out the window one afternoon and said, "Sally and Jane certainly look happy and excited." What might have made the girls so excited? (**party, trip, present**)

3. How many games can you name that use a ball? (**football, basketball, racquetball**) That use a racket or some type of stick? (**hockey, golf, tennis**)

4. "I don't think I'm ever going to learn to play ball," moaned Josh to his friend, Tom. Tom said, "I think I know what you should do." What might he have had in mind? (**The two of them practice together, get a friend or parent to help, consider a different sport for which Josh is more suited**)

5. If you heard your cat meowing, but couldn't see him, where might he be? (**caught in a closet, outside the window, in a box**)

6. "That package is from Grandmother, I bet," said Karen when she saw the mail carrier walking up the sidewalk. Why might she have said this? (**Her birthday is soon. Her grandmother had written a letter saying a package was on the way. Her grandmother had told her to watch for a surprise.**)

7. "I'm afraid a bear has been in our campsite," said Dad. What might have caused him to say this? (**people standing around looking, things spilled, footprints**)

8. Lines are used for many different purposes. Where have you seen lines and why were they used? (on a highway to show where the edge of the road was, to mark the boundaries of a football field, at school to show where to line up)

9. What might make you think the temperature was cooler, when the temperature hadn't really changed? (clouds, humidity lower, more wind)

10. There are many different kinds of safety signs, such as stop signs or yield signs. What other safety signs can you name? (slow, caution, one way)

11. How are station wagons and pickup trucks alike? (both haul things, provide transportation, use gasoline) How are they different? (size; a pickup is open in the back and a station wagon is closed; the truck can haul much larger things than the station wagon)

12. "Someone had honey in this measuring cup," said Judy. But she hadn't seen anyone use the cup. How might she have known? (saw honey inside, felt the stickiness, saw the drips down the side of the cup)

13. What could you find out by looking at a menu in a restaurant? (what types of foods are served, prices, whether there is a chidren's menu)

14. How might you know someone had been injured? (see the person limping, see people standing around the person, see an ambulance arrive)

15. What are some indications that Spring has arrived? (warmer weather, trees and flowers budding, migrating birds returning)

16. "Now that I've moved to the city, I don't use my car as much as I used to," said Mr. Thompson. Why would this be? (has a difficult time finding a place to park, prefers to take the bus or subway, doesn't like to drive in heavy traffic)

17. "Jimmy's dog will do tricks for him, but he won't do them for me," said Mike. What could be the reason for this? (The dog doesn't like Mike. Jimmy was the person who trained the dog. Jimmy gives the dog a reward when he does tricks and Mike doesn't reward him.)

18. Boy Scouts and Girl Scouts are supposed to do a good deed every day. What are some good deeds you have done? (entertain a younger child, help with chores, help carry groceries into the house)

19. If you had a dog and were going to move into an apartment that did not allow dogs, what could you do? (Ask a relative to keep the dog for you; take it to an animal shelter; talk to the manager and explain that your dog would not bark and would not damage anything in the apartment.)

20. How could you know that a cup of hot chocolate was hot, without sipping it? (see steam, see someone fixing it, feel the outside of the cup)

21. What places require an admission fee? (zoo, amusement park, movie, museum)

22. "I think I'm coming down with a cold," said Shiela as she walked home from school with her friend, Carol. What might have made her say this? (sore throat, feels like she has a fever, nose is stopped up)

23. How are a motorcycle and a wheelchair alike? (provide transportation, have wheels, you sit on them) How are they different? (different number of wheels; one travels on the street and the other on the sidewalk; one can be driven inside of buildings)

24. "I didn't know you were going to be taking a trip, Dad," said Troy. What might have caused him to think this? (saw suitcases out, saw tickets, heard his father talking to the travel agent)

25. Frank said to Susan as they were walking across a meadow, "Lots of people like to picnic here." Yet there was no one having a picnic in the meadow. Why might he have said this? (**grass matted, charred wood from barbecue fires, cans and bottles left around or in the trash cans**)

26. How could you know it rained, even though you didn't see it rain? (**see puddles, hear thunder, smell clean fresh air**)

27. "Janie, I wish you wouldn't get into my perfume," said Mother. But Mother had not seen Janie use the perfume. How might she have known? (**smell, bottle in a different location, cap left off bottle**)

28. If you were on an airplane, how might you know that it would be landing soon? (**pilot says, "Fasten your seatbelts." feel plane descending, ears popping**)

REPRODUCIBLE ACTIVITY PAGE (GRADES 3–6)

If this activity is used with the entire class, distribute the reproducible page and briefly discuss its format. After students have had time to complete the page, have them share their answers. Discuss the diversity of their thinking and have them share additional ideas that occur to them as they listen to the thoughts of others.

Answer Key: Sample answers follow, but any answer that can be backed by logical reasoning should be accepted. (1) She heard the train whistle; she had seen the train approaching; she saw traffic backed up at the railroad crossing. (2) The road was flooded; there was going to be a parade; repairs were being made. (3) She heard a strange sound coming from the washing machine; she saw bubbles spilling out of the machine; she heard the machine stop long before the cycle was finished.

HOW MANY ANSWERS CAN YOU FIND?

Read the following questions. Write three possible answers for each question.

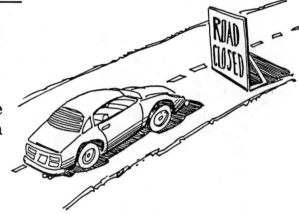

"A train is about to go through that railroad crossing," said Julie to her mother. What might have made her say this?

1. _____

2. _____

3. _____

The sign said, "ROAD CLOSED TO TRAFFIC." What could the reason have been?

1. _____

2. _____

3. _____

"Oh no! There's something wrong with the washing machine again," exclaimed Mrs. Jackson. What might have caused her to say this?

1. _____

2. _____

3. _____

12 HERE'S THE ANSWER— WHAT WAS THE QUESTION?

Materials needed:

☒ reproducible page
☒ total group activity
☒ individual activity
☐ partner activity

TOTAL GROUP ACTIVITY

This activity is the opposite of what usually happens in the classroom. Explain to students that you will give them the *answer* to a question, and they are to think of the questions that might have resulted in this answer. For each of the answers you read, there will be several possible questions that could have been asked. Sample questions are provided here. For example, if the answer is "my birthday," the question might have been:

— What is your favorite day of the year?
— What will next Monday be?

Give several examples before starting this activity so students become accustomed to thinking "in reverse."

ADAPTATION FOR AN INDIVIDUAL STUDENT (GRADES 3–6)

Materials needed:

lined paper (6″ × 9″ for class book)
pencil

The student writes an answer that could be given in response to a variety of questions. On the reverse side of the paper, the student lists two or three questions that might have been asked. When a sufficient number of these papers have been collected, they can be assembled into an interesting class book to be used individually or as a total group activity.

Here's the Answer— What Was the Question?

1. my lunch

What just spilled all over the floor? What did you lose? What did you just eat?

39

2. a ball

What did you take outside at recess? What does your dog like to play with? What did you buy at the store?

3. my cat

What made that sound? What do you sleep with? What just ran up that tree?

4. on Saturday

When do you get to stay up late? When do you do your chores? When are you going to the movie?

5. after lunch

When are we going shopping? When are you supposed to call your mother? When does your little sister take a nap?

6. a dog

What would you like for your birthday? What is that behind the fence? What made that sound?

7. Let's ask.

What are we going to have for dinner tonight? When are we going to get to go outside? How long does the movie last?

8. cartoons

What makes you laugh? What do you watch on Saturday mornings? What's on TV right now?

9. after dinner

When do you do your homework? When do you want to take a walk? When is your friend going home?

10. my mom

Who mowed the grass? Who is picking you up after school? Who woke you up this morning?

11. when it snows

When do you build a snowman? When do you like to sit in front of a fire? When are snowplows used?

12. on my desk

Where is the dictionary? Where did you put your homework? Where is the cat?

13. on Thanksgiving

When do you usually eat turkey? When are your grandparents coming to visit? When will the parade be on television?

14. in the closet

Where is the mouse? Where did you put my coat? Where is Jim hiding?

15. a guitar

What is your favorite instrument? What instrument does your sister play? What is that instrument?

16. my best friend

Who do you want to win the race? Who is that climbing over the fence? Who is going to help you with your math?

17. You're kidding!

Did you know we won first prize in the contest? Did you hear that it's supposed to rain on the day we've planned the picnic? Did you know Jim is moving to Oklahoma?

18. soon

When will the party begin? When will it be time for lunch? When do you think it will start raining?

19. California

Where is Disneyland? Where did you go on your vacation? Where does your friend live?

20. my neighbor

Who knocked down the tree in the front yard? Who is going to take care of your dog while you are gone? Who owns that new car?

21. in the ocean

Where did you catch that fish? Where did you go scuba diving? Where does the largest mammal in the world live?

22. stop

What do you do at a red light? What do you say when someone is tickling you? What does that sign say?

23. He fell down.   Why did he quit running in the race? What happened when your little brother started to walk? What happened when Jim got to the top of the jungle gym?

24. in the garden   Where did that rabbit go? Where did you plant the seeds? Where is your dad?

25. next to the house   Where is the swing set? Where did you put your bike? Where did your dog bury the bone?

REPRODUCIBLE ACTIVITY PAGE (GRADES 3–6)

If this activity is used with the entire class, distribute the reproducible page and briefly discuss its format. After students have had time to complete the page, have them share their answers. Discuss the diversity of their thinking and have them share additional ideas that occur to them as they listen to the thoughts of others.

Answer Key: Sample answers follow, but any answer that can be backed by logical reasoning should be accepted. (1) *on the playground:* Where did you play hopscotch? Where did you find that ball? Where did you break your arm? (2) *No!* Would you like liver and spinach for dinner? Is that your dog who just bit the mail carrier? Do you like doing chores? (3) *my brother:* Who wakes you up every morning? Who is that little boy who is pulling the cat's tail? Who just hit the homerun? (4) *mud:* What is something that's squishy? What is all over your clothes? What made the tracks all over the carpet?

HERE'S THE ANSWER—WHAT WAS THE QUESTION?

Here are some *answers* to questions. For each answer,
write *two questions* that might have been asked.

ANSWER	WHAT COULD THE QUESTION HAVE BEEN?
my birthday	1. What is your favorite day of the year? 2. What will next Monday be?
on the playground	1. _____ 2. _____
No!	1. _____ 2. _____
my brother	1. _____ 2. _____
mud	1. _____ 2. _____

13 ANALOGIES

Materials needed:

☒ reproducible page
☒ total group activity
☒ individual activity
☐ partner activity

TOTAL GROUP ACTIVITY

Analogies are often baffling to children because they do not have a systematic approach to solving them. For instance, you may present the analogy:

Dog is to fur as
Bird is to _____,

and a child may answer, "fly." The student has established a relationship, but not the correct one.

The following approach guides students through the necessary thinking steps. Once students understand how to work analogies they become successful and very excited about them. This invariably results in analogies becoming one of their favorite thinking activities.

Procedure: Explain to students that they are going to play a game using words that go together. Say a pair of words and then say the first word of a second pair. They are to act as detectives and try to find the missing word.

Explain that the "clue" is to discover why and **how** the first pair go together. Give the example:

Grass is to green as
Sky is to _____.

Ask what makes grass and green go together. When it's determined that the color of grass is green, explain that the way to complete the second pair is to ask yourself, "If grass is green, then what color is the sky?"

Read the first word pair of another analogy:

Milk is to glass

Ask how these words go together. When it's determined that a glass is a container that holds milk, give them the second pair:

Milk is to glass as

soup is to _____. **(bowl)**

Once the correct answer has been given, summarize the thinking process:

"A glass is a container that holds milk.
Ask yourself, 'What is a container that holds soup?'... Bowl.
Therefore, milk is to glass as soup is to bowl."

Continue in this manner, guiding them through several analogies, each time having them clarify the relationship of the first words before attempting to complete the analogy.

When they are confident of the procedure, read an analogy, omitting the final word. Each time a student gives a correct answer, acknowledge that it is correct. Then have the student explain how the first words were related and how this led to the answer. This continuously reinforces the process for those children who are less secure.

If an incorrect answer is given, help the child go back through the thinking process: "How do the first words go together?" and so on.

In the following analogies, one answer is given in parentheses. However, any answer that maintains a logical relationship should be accepted.

ADAPTATION FOR AN INDIVIDUAL STUDENT (GRADES 3–6)

Materials needed:

unlined paper (6″ × 9″ for class book)
pencil

The student writes as many analogies as he or she can think of. These can later be used as a challenge for the whole class. Or the student can write each analogy on a separate piece of 6″ × 9″ paper, omitting the answer on the front and writing it with an illustration, if desired, on the reverse side.

When a sufficient number of these papers have been collected, they can be assembled into a thought-provoking class puzzle book.

Complete These Analogies

1. Tomato is to red as lemon is to _____ (yellow).
2. Train is to tracks as boat is to _____ (water).
3. Elephant is to large as mouse is to _____ (small).
4. Winter is to cold as summer is to _____ (hot).
5. Fish is to swim as rabbit is to _____ (hop).
6. Glove is to hand as shoe is to _____ (foot).
7. Hamburger is to eat as milkshake is to _____ (drink).

8. Bird is to chirp as cat is to _____ (meow).

9. Apple is to fruit as carrot is to _____ (vegetable).

10. Sun is to day as moon is to _____ (night).

11. Roof is to house as hat is to _____ (head).

12. Robin is to worm as horse is to _____ (grass).

13. Laughter is to happiness as tears are to _____ (sadness).

14. Bacon is to fry as cookies are to _____ (bake).

15. Tablecloth is to table as carpet is to _____ (floor).

16. Cake is to fork as ice cream is to _____ (spoon).

17. Honey is to sticky as ice is to _____ (slippery).

18. Loud is to scream as soft is to _____ (whisper).

19. Kangaroo is to hop as snake is to _____ (slither).

20. Hamburger is to cattle as bacon is to _____ (pigs).

21. Taste is to mouth as sight is to _____ (eyes).

22. Knee is to leg as elbow is to _____ (arm).

23. Dishwasher is to dishes as washing machine is to _____ (clothes).

24. Noon is to lunch as morning is to _____ (breakfast).

25. Wide is to narrow as high is to _____ (low).

26. Stove is to appliance as chair is to _____ (furniture).

27. Football is to field as tennis is to _____ (court).

28. Rough is to smooth as crooked is to _____ (straight).

29. Whale is to mammal as ant is to _____ (insect).

30. Far is to near as shut is to _____ (open).

31. Chimney is to roof as flag is to _____ (flagpole).

32. Water is to submarine as air is to _____ (airplane).

33. Grape is to raisin as prune is to _____ (plum).

34. Mountain is to high as valley is to _____ (low).

35. War is to peace as hate is to _____ (love).

36. Chicago is to city as United States is to _____ (country).

37. Shark is to ocean as scorpion is to _____ (desert).

38. President is to country as governor is to _____ (state).

39. Brook is to narrow as river is to _____ (wide).

40. Walk is to slow as dash is to _____ (fast).

41. Copper is to mineral as oxygen is to _____ (gas).

42. Fish are to school as cattle are to _____ (herd).

43. Peel is to potato as husk is to _____ (corn).

44. Pen is to letter as printing is to _____ (book).

45. Bad is to good as innocent is to _____ (guilty).

REPRODUCIBLE ACTIVITY PAGE (GRADES 4–6)

If this activity is used with the entire class, distribute the reproducible page and briefly discuss its format. After students have had time to complete the page, have them share their answers. Discuss the diversity of their thinking and have them share additional ideas that occur to them as they listen to the thoughts of others.

Answer Key: Answers will vary.

ANALOGIES

Analogies are word pairs that go together in a special way. The first step in writing an analogy is to choose two words that go together in some way. For example the words *loud* and *scream* have to do with the amount of sound, in this case loud sound. The next step is to think of two other words that compare the amount of sound, but not loud sounds: *soft* and *whisper* would work well. The analogy would then be:

Loud is to scream as
soft is to whisper.

1. Write an analogy that compares the color of objects.

   Yellow is to lemon as

   _____ is to _____ .

2. Write an analogy that compares the way animals move.

   Hop is to _____ as

   _____ is to _____ .

3. Write an analogy that compares the way things feel.

   Rough is to _____ as

   _____ is to _____ .

4. Write an analogy that compares times of day.

   Noon is to _____ as

   _____ is to _____ .

5. Now write your own analogy.

   _____ is to _____ as

   _____ is to _____ .

---

14   PROVERBS

Materials needed:

☒ reproducible page
☒ total group activity
☒ individual activity
☐ partner activity

TOTAL GROUP ACTIVITY

Explain to students that a proverb is generally a short sentence which tells a truth or a helpful bit of wisdom. Most proverbs are quite old and have been handed down from generation to generation. All languages have proverbs, and the same thought is often expressed in several different languages. The meaning of some proverbs is clearly stated, "Haste makes waste," for example. However, many proverbs can be interpreted both literally and in a broader context. "It's too late to lock the barn door after the horse is gone," is certainly a true statement, but in a broader interpretation it indicates that when a task is delayed, a time may come when it's too late to do anything about it.

Read the following proverbs and have the students explain each of them. In some cases, leading questions may need to be asked to help clarify the broader interpretation.

ADAPTATION FOR AN INDIVIDUAL STUDENT (GRADES 3–6)

Materials needed:

unlined paper (9″ × 12″ for class book)
pencil
crayons

Have a student or volunteer copy the following proverbs on pieces of 9″ × 12″ paper (one per page). Individual students may select one of the papers and illustrate the meaning of the proverb. When all papers have been completed, assemble them into a class book, to be enjoyed by all.

As an alternate follow-up activity, have individual students use books of proverbs to research the origins of these sayings.

What Do Each of These Proverbs Mean?

1. Haste makes waste.
2. Where there's a will, there's a way.
3. A stitch in time saves nine.
4. Out of sight, out of mind.
5. There's no use crying over spilled milk.
6. Don't count your chickens before they hatch.

7. Practice makes perfect.

8. Look before you leap.

9. Two wrongs don't make a right.

10. Don't bite off more than you can chew.

11. Honesty is the best policy.

12. Nothing ventured, nothing gained.

13. You can lead a horse to water, but you can't make it drink.

14. You can't have your cake and eat it too.

15. No news is good news.

16. From little acorns, big oaks grow.

17. The only way to have a friend is to be one.

18. Many hands make light work.

19. Live and let live.

20. Curiosity killed the cat.

21. Better late than never.

22. Everything has its beauty, but not everyone sees it.

23. Don't cross your bridges until you come to them.

24. Birds of a feather flock together.

25. Saying and doing are two different things.

26. It's too late to lock the barn door after the horse is gone.

27. A word to the wise is sufficient.

28. What is said cannot be unsaid.

29. All that glitters is not gold.

30. Don't put all your eggs in one basket.

31. Actions speak louder than words.

32. Every cloud has a silver lining.

33. A penny saved is a penny earned.

34. The early bird catches the worm.

35. Once bitten, twice shy.

REPRODUCIBLE ACTIVITY PAGE (GRADES 2–4)

Answer Key: Answers will vary.

PROVERBS

Where there's a will, there's a way!

Proverbs are well-known sayings that tell a truth or give some bit of useful advice.

Read the following proverbs and explain what you think each one means.

Haste makes waste.

_____

_____

_____

Where there's a will, there's a way.

_____

_____

_____

Honesty is the best policy.

_____

_____

_____

Many hands make light work.

_____

_____

_____

15   FLOWCHARTS

Materials needed:

chalk
chalkboard

☒ reproducible page
☒ total group activity
☐ individual activity
☐ partner activity

TOTAL GROUP ACTIVITY

Explain to students that flowcharts are a way to diagram or show the sequential steps and decisions that need to be made in order to complete a task. They are often used in connection with computer programming. Discuss the following symbols:

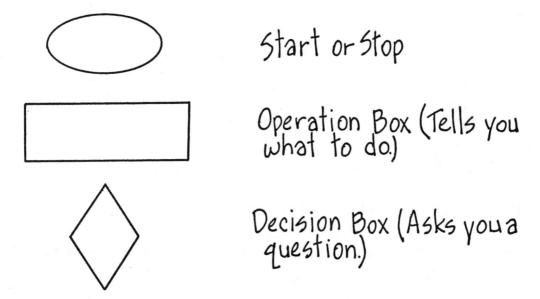

Start or Stop

Operation Box (Tells you what to do.)

Decision Box (Asks you a question.)

As a simple warm-up activity, have students work together to design a flow chart showing how to select a cold cereal at the grocery store. Diagram the chart on the chalkboard as they make suggestions. Provide guidance as needed, and encourage them to ask questions and to evaluate their plan in terms of whether it does what it is intended to do, and whether it could be simplified in any way. The final chart might look something like the one on the following page.

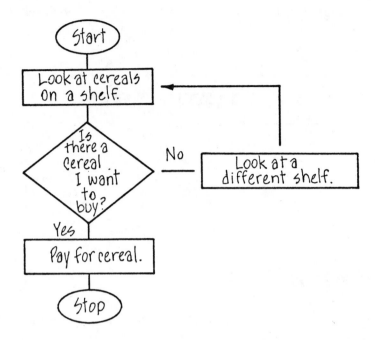

Other topics that make interesting flowcharts include:

1. planting a tree
2. how to check a book out of the library
3. washing dishes
4. building a campfire
5. how to wash a dog
6. making a cup of hot chocolate
7. how to roller skate
8. choosing a TV program

REPRODUCIBLE ACTIVITY PAGE (GRADES 3–6)

Answer Key: Answers will vary. A sample flow chart follows, but any answer that can be backed by logical reasoning should be accepted.

One Possible Solution

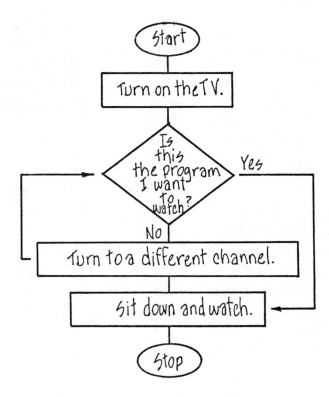

Suggestion: If you do not have time to duplicate the reproducible page, as an alterante procedure write one of the above topics on the chalkboard and have students work alone or with partners to design a flow chart.

FLOWCHARTS

Flowcharts show what steps or decisions need to be taken in order to complete a task.

Look at the flowchart at the top of this page. Then study the symbols to the right. These are the three main symbols that are used in making flowcharts.

Now it's your turn! Draw a flowchart that shows someone how to select a TV program by changing channels until they find the program they want. Then have them sit down and watch it. Be sure to end your flowchart with the STOP symbol.

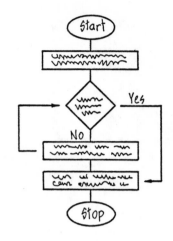

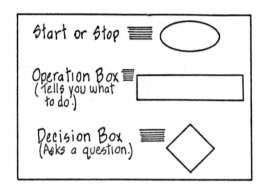

Start or Stop

Operation Box
(Tells you what to do.)

Decision Box
(Asks a question.)

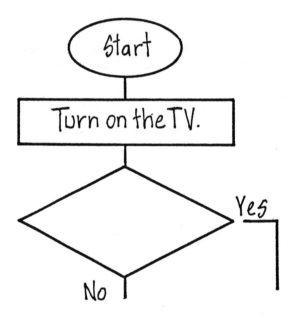

Start

Turn on the TV.

Yes

No

16   WHO/WHAT AM I?

Materials needed:

pencil
lined paper

☒ reproducible page
☒ total group activity
☐ individual activity
☒ partner activity

TOTAL GROUP ACTIVITY

Students select a famous person, place, or object and write four or five clues about its identity. They should start with broad clues and make each successive clue more explicit.

Example:

1. I am a well-known place.
2. You'd find me on the west coast of the United States.
3. I am a state.
4. If you came to visit me, you could go to Disneyland.
5. The Golden Gate Bridge is one of my famous landmarks.

(*Answer*: California)

Have a student read his or her clues, allowing others to guess after each clue is read. The person who guesses the correct answer begins the next "Who/What Am I?" riddle.

PARTNER ADAPTATION (GRADES 4–6)

Working with a partner, students follow the above procedure. When a student guesses the identity of the person, place, or thing, one point is earned for each clue remaining on the opponent's list. Play continues for a designated time period or until one of the players has ten points.

This can easily be made a "silent partner activity," by having the player who is "It" *show* one clue at a time to the other player. This player then *writes* his or her guess. Play continues as above.

REPRODUCIBLE ACTIVITY PAGE (GRADES 4–6)

If this activity is used with the entire class, distribute the reproducible page and briefly discuss its format. After students have had time to complete the page, have them share their answers. Discuss the diversity of their thinking and have them share additional ideas that occur to them as they listen to the thoughts of others.

Answer Key: Sample answers follow, but any answer that can be backed by logical reasoning should be accepted. *Statue of Liberty:* (1) You can find me on the east coast of America. (2) I am an object that is known all over the world. (3) If you were coming into New York harbor by boat, I would be one of the first things you would see. (4) People have thought of me as a symbol of freedom for over one hundred years. *Great Wall of China:* (1) I was built to keep out invaders. (2) I am a famous place in China. (3) You could walk on me. (4) I am a wall. *King Tut:* (1) I am a famous person, even though I am dead. (2) I was a King but I died when I was still young. (3) A lot of treasures were buried with me. (4) I lived in Egypt.

NAME _____

WHO/WHAT AM I?

Write a four-clue riddle about each famous person, place, or object listed below. Start with a clue that won't give the answer away. Each clue should give a little more information. The final clue should provide the most help in solving the riddle. For example, here are four clues. (1) I am a well-known place. (2) I am a state. (3) If you came to visit me, you could go to Disneyland. (4) The Golden Gate Bridge is one of my famous landmarks. (Answer: California)

Here is the answer to a riddle: *Statue of Liberty.* What are the clues?

1. _____

2. _____

3. _____

4. _____

Here is the answer to a riddle: *Great Wall of China.* What are the clues?

1. _____

2. _____

3. _____

4. _____

Here is the answer to a riddle: *King Tut.* What are the clues?

1. _____

2. _____

3. _____

4. _____

17 WHAT-WOULD-YOU-DO? STORIES

Materials needed:

☐ reproducible page
☒ total group activity
☐ individual activity
☐ partner activity

TOTAL GROUP ACTIVITY

Read each of the following stories and then ask the students what they think the person might do. Encourage a variety of solutions and discussion about the possible consequences of each solution.

A. My Friends Are Calling a Classmate Names…(Grades 2–6)

Katie heard the recess bell ring, but she wanted to finish the math problem she was working on. There were just a couple of more numbers to write. As she put her pencil down, she heard Lisa calling to her from the doorway, "Hurry up, Katie, or we're not going to have any time for recess." Katie grabbed her coat and hurried to the door, where her friends Lisa and Joan were waiting for her. The three of them always played together at recess and after school. In fact her dad teasingly called them "the inseparable three."

As they walked down the hallway, they passed Anne. Katie felt sorry for Anne. She never had anyone to play with and the other kids always made fun of her behind her back. But today was even worse. As they passed Anne, Lisa and Joan started talking about her and calling her names. Katie was sure that Anne could hear them talking, and it made her feel very uncomfortable.

That night at dinner, she said something to her parents about what had happened. Her mom said, "Katie, couldn't you be a friend to Anne? How would you feel if people treated you that way?"

Katie kept thinking about what her mom had said, but she also kept thinking about how much she liked Lisa and Joan and about all the fun they'd had together. What if she were nice to Anne, and Lisa and Joan started making fun of her?

The next day at lunch recess, the three girls had just started to play a game when a voice behind them said, "Hi. Could I play too?" Katie looked up, and there was Anne.

What might Katie do?

B. How Come He's Always Bossing Me Around?…(Grades 2–6)

Jimmy heard his friend, Mike, outside shouting, "Hurry up Jimmy. Come on out and get your bike. I swear you're the slowest person I ever knew."

Mike was a couple of years older than Jimmy, but they played together almost every day. Jimmy grabbed his coat, ran to get his bike and called to Mike, "Where are we going?" "We're going to go up to school and ride around on the playground," shouted Mike as he went racing down the sidewalk. Jimmy pedaled as fast as he could, trying his best to keep up with Mike.

After they had ridden around the playground for a while, Jimmy said, "I've got an idea. Let's weave in and out of all the things on the playground." "No," said Mike, "Let's make a motocross course. We'll pretend the things on the playground are part of the course and that we have to steer around them. Then we can pretend the curbs are logs that we have to jump over. Hey, if we think about it, this could be a really neat course."

Mike got busy figuring out the motocross course and telling Jimmy what they'd have to do at each place along the way. Every time Jimmy had an idea, Mike would say, "Nah, that wouldn't be any good. What we'll do is..." and then Mike would say the way he wanted it."

Finally Jimmy said, "Mike, how come it always has to be your way? Why can't we use some of my ideas? You know I have good ideas too!" Mike just laughed and said, "No way. Your ideas are baby ideas. I'm laying this out like a real motocross course."

Jimmy could feel the blood rush to his face. He felt angry, but he didn't say anything.

When Mike's motocross course was finished he said, "O.K. let's race." They raced for what seemed like a long time to Jimmy. Finally Jimmy said, "I've got an idea. Let's take our bikes over to the park and coast down the hill."

Right away Mike said in a whining kind of voice, "Ah, you want to quit, huh? I'm too good for you. You just don't like getting beat. That's O.K. Go on and quit."

Jimmy was mad. He thought, "Why does Mike always make fun of me and go bossing me around? Everything always has to be the way *he* wants it? I really don't want to drive around his old motocross course anymore. But if I leave I won't have anyone to play with."

What could Jimmy do?

C. Decisions, Decisions...(Grades 3–6)

Jennifer and her family had moved to a new town during the summer. At first she had been excited about the move and especially about having a bedroom all for herself. But now they were all settled in the new house, and Jennifer really missed her old friends. She kept hoping some of the girls in the neighborhood would invite her to play, but so far no one had.

One night as her dad was reading the newspaper, he mentioned that there was going to be a computer class starting the next week. Jennifer had been fascinated with the computer at her old school and had begged to take a class, but her parents had said the classes were too expensive. To her surprise, her dad looked up from his paper and said, "Jennifer, would you like me to sign you up for this course?" Jennifer thought that was the very best thing she'd heard in a long while.

The next night when her dad came home from work he said he'd enrolled her in the class and that it was very important she go to the first meeting. He explained that if there weren't enough people at the first meeting, the course would be canceled. Jennifer said, "You don't have to worry about me missing the class. I can't wait!"

Finally the day for the computer class arrived. Her parents reminded her as they left for work that she should be there at 2:00 o'clock.

Just after lunch there was a knock on the door. Jennifer couldn't believe it when she saw the person at the door was the girl from down the street. She told Jennifer that her name was Sally and that she and some of her friends were going to a movie that afternoon. They wondered if Jennifer would like to go with them. Jennifer thought, "Oh no. If I don't go to the computer class the rest of the sessions are liable to be canceled. And besides, if I tell dad I didn't go, I don't think he'll sign me up for another class. But I want to go to the movie with Sally and her friends so much."

What might Jennifer do?

D. He's Cheating!...(Grades 3–6)

Adam knew that the math test was going to be on Friday and that if he did well on it, he might be able to pull his grade up to a B. His teacher had given everyone some practice pages and suggested that they work on the problems during the week to help them review for the test.

On Tuesday night there was a program on television that Adam really wanted to see. "That's O.K.," he thought. "I'll study tomorrow night." But just as he sat down to dinner on Wednesday, his good friend, Steve called and said, "My dad came home with some tickets for the big football game. He has one extra ticket, and he said I could invite you to come along." What a break! That was a really important game, and here was his chance to see it. He thought, "If I go tonight, I'll still have tomorrow to study. That will be enough time if I come home from school and get right to work." So off he went to the game.

As soon as he walked in the house Thursday afternoon, he heard his mom calling to him from the bedroom. One look at her told him that something was wrong.

"I've come down with a bad case of the flu," she moaned. "I have a high temperature, and I feel just terrible. Mrs. Frederick has been watching the baby all day, but I told her you'd come get him as soon as you got home. I'm sorry, but you're going to have to take care of him until he goes to bed tonight. You know your dad is out of town, so you're going to be on your own."

Adam thought, "Oh no!" But he realized that he had no choice. Finally when he got the baby to sleep, he tried to study. But it was late, and he was just too sleepy. After a while he gave up and went to bed.

The next day his friends were all talking about the test and how they'd studied for it. Adam thought, "I've got to do well on this test. But what am I going to do?"

As soon as everyone was in the room the teacher handed out the test. It didn't take Adam long to realize there were a lot of problems he couldn't solve. Then he noticed that if he moved his chair just a little to the side he could see Jason's paper, and he knew that Jason always did well on math tests. By glancing at Jason's paper every now and then, he was able to work a lot of the problems he had previously skipped. As Adam was just about to finish the test, Jason got up and walked to the teacher's desk. To Adam's horror he heard Jason tell the teacher that Adam had been looking at his test and copying his answers.

What might Adam do?

18 FOUR IN A ROW

Materials needed:

unlined paper or graph paper
pencil
Optional: ruler

☐ reproducible page
☐ total group activity
☐ individual activity
☒ partner activity

PARTNER ACTIVITY

This activity provides practice in developing strategy skills. Students may use graph paper as a gameboard, or they may make their own gameboard by using unlined paper and drawing from ten to twenty lines down and ten to twenty lines across.

One player writes "X"s and the other player writes "O"s. The first person makes an "X" in the center of the playing area. The players then take turns writing their mark above, below, or to either side of any "X" or "O" on the board. (Marks may not be made in diagonally adjacent boxes.)

The first player to get four of his or her marks in a row, vertically or horizontally, wins the game.

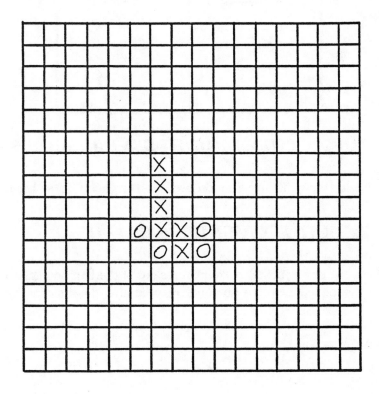

19   SQUIGGLE IMAGINATION

Materials needed:

unlined paper for each student
pencil
optional: crayons

☒ reproducible page
☐ total group activity
☒ individual activity
☒ partner activity

PARTNER ACTIVITY

Each of the partners folds a piece of paper into four squares, traces over the folds with a pencil, and draws a "squiggle in each square.

The partners then trade papers and attempt to turn each of the squiggles into a picture.

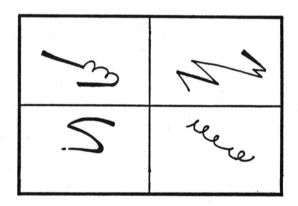

ADAPTATION FOR AN INDIVIDUAL STUDENT (GRADES K–6)

The student should follow the above procedure, but then keep his or her own paper.

REPRODUCIBLE ACTIVITY PAGE (GRADES 1–4)

Students use crayons or a pencil to make pictures out of the four squiggles on the reproducible page. Display the completed work so students may admire the imaginative solutions of their classmates.

Answer Key: Answers will vary.

SQUIGGLE IMAGINATION

Look at the four squiggles below. Use a pencil or crayons and turn each squiggle into a picture.

20   TWO BY TWO STRATEGY

Materials needed:

unlined paper
pencil
optional: ruler

☒ reproducible page
☐ total group activity
☒ individual activity
☒ partner activity

PARTNER ACTIVITY

This activity provides practice in developing strategies.

Students draw a zigzag playing board, varying the number of squares from game to game. They take turns writing one or two "X"s in *adjacent* squares, anywhere on the board.

The last person to mark *two* adjacent squares is the winner. Students should be encouraged to develop game strategies.

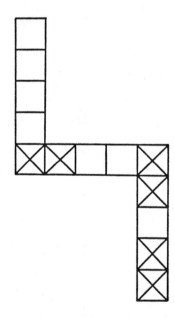

ADAPTATION FOR AN INDIVIDUAL STUDENT (GRADES 2–6)

An individual student can practice strategies for winning the game by following the above procedure and using two different colors of pencils, pens, or crayons to represent the two players.

REPRODUCIBLE ACTIVITY PAGE (GRADES 2–6)

Students follow the rules on the previous page, using the four "gameboards" provided on the reproducible page.

Answer Key: Answers will vary.

TWO BY TWO STRATEGY

There are four different gameboards below. Play these games with a partner, or you may play against yourself by using two different colors of crayons, pencils, or pens. One color stands for you and the other for your opponent.

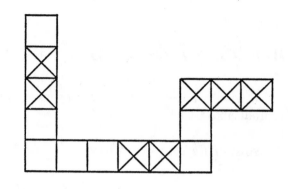

Choose a gameboard and play until there is a winner. Then use a new gameboard. The rules are the same for all the games.

Take turns writing one or two "X"s in *adjacent* squares, anywhere on the gameboard.

The last person to mark *two* adjacent squares is the winner.

21   ABC CATEGORIES

Materials needed:
4 pieces of 8 ½″ × 11″ paper
pencil
optional: crayons

☒ reproducible page
☐ total group activity
☒ individual activity
☐ partner activity

INDIVIDUAL ACTIVITY

The student selects a topic that is of special interest, or you may assign a topic from the list below. Fold four pieces of 8½″ × 11″ paper into eight equal sections. Unfold the papers and staple them together. The title of the selected topic, the student's name, and a few representative illustrations are written in the top two sections. The alphabet is written sequentially in the remaining sections, one letter per box. (Two sections will be left over.)

The student then thinks of words within the chosen category that begin with each letter of the alphabet and completes as many sections as possible with an appropriate word and illustration: A is for _____, B is for _____, and so on.

Alphabetical Categories

animals
foods
items you can buy, other than food
things in the classroom
topics of special interest to student
words associated with holidays
occupations
words that go with sports
words that describe a person

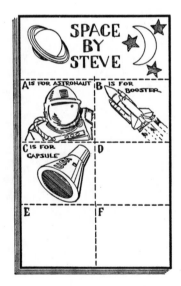

REPRODUCIBLE ACTIVITY PAGE (GRADES 2–6)

Answer Key: Answers will vary.

ABC CATEGORIES

Think of a topic that is of special interest to you,
or choose one from the list below.

animals	things in the classroom
items that you can buy, other than food	words that go with sports
foods	words that describe a person

Write your topic in the box. Then think of words that
begin with each letter of the alphabet and that go with
your topic. Use these words to fill in as many spaces as
you can. For example, if your topic were space, you
might write: "A is for astronaut, B is for booster . . ."

A is for _____   N is for _____

B is for _____   O is for _____

C is for _____   P is for _____

D is for _____   Q is for _____

E is for _____   R is for _____

F is for _____   S is for _____

G is for _____   T is for _____

H is for _____   U is for _____

I is for _____   V is for _____

J is for _____   W is for _____

K is for _____   X is for _____

L is for _____   Y is for _____

M is for _____   Z is for _____

22 WHAT'S THE SEQUENCE?

Materials needed:

lined paper (6″ × 9″ for class book)
pencil

☒ reproducible page
☐ total group activity
☒ individual activity
☐ partner activity

INDIVIDUAL ACTIVITY

The student thinks of four words that can be sequenced in some way and then writes a clue that challenges others to try to think of four words, either the same as the student's or a different series, that could be sequenced in the same manner. For example, the student might write: Think of four fruits that could be sequenced from smallest to largest. One possible solution should be written on the back side of the paper (Example: cherry, lemon, grapefruit, watermelon).

To help the student get started, suggest different ways items can be sorted: size, stages of development (people, animals, plants), words that denote time, linear measurement or volume, and so on. This is also a good time to suggest that the student use vocabulary words that relate to his or her own special interests or words that correlate with current units of study.

When a sufficient number of papers have been collected, they can be assembled into a thought-provoking class puzzle book for individual or whole-class use.

Think of four holidays
that could be sequenced
from the beginning of
the year to the end of
the year.

_____ , _____ , _____ , _____

Front

≡≡ One Solution ≡≡

New Year's Day,
Easter,
Fourth of July,
Thanksgiving

Back

REPRODUCIBLE ACTIVITY PAGE (GRADES 2–4)

Answer Key: Sample answers follow, but any answer that can be backed by logical reasoning should be accepted. (1) day, week, month, year—length of time; (2) baby, child, teenager, adult—age; (3) grape, lemon, orange, watermelon—size; (4) cup, pint, quart, gallon—volume; (5) Answers will vary.

NAME _____

WHAT'S THE SEQUENCE?

Read each group of words below. Think of a way that you can write them so that they are in order. Then use the words in the *WORD BANK* to tell how you sequenced them.

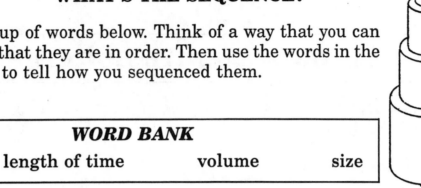

WORD BANK			
age	length of time	volume	size

THINK OF A WAY TO PUT THESE WORDS IN ORDER

1. | year, day, month, week |

_____ , _____ , _____ , _____

How were the words sequenced? _____

2. | baby, teenager, child, adult |

_____ , _____ , _____ , _____

How were the words sequenced? _____

3. | watermelon, orange, grape, lemon |

_____ , _____ , _____ , _____

How were the words sequenced? _____

4. | pint, gallon, cup, quart |

_____ , _____ , _____ , _____

How were the words sequenced? _____

5. | Now it's your turn. Write four NEW words in sequence. |

_____ , _____ , _____ , _____

How were the words sequenced? _____

23 OBJECTS WITH BODY PARTS

Materials needed:

paper (6″ x 9″ for class book)
pencil
Optional: crayons

☒ reproducible page
☐ total group activity
☒ individual activity
☐ partner activity

INDIVIDUAL ACTIVITY

The student thinks of objects that have parts with names that are the same as names of parts of our bodies. For example, we have teeth, and a zipper has teeth.

On a piece of 6″ x 9″ paper, two pictures are drawn side by side, showing the object and a person. The student writes at the bottom of the paper: "What do a person and a _____ have in common?" The answer is then written on the back of the paper.

When a sufficient number of papers have been collected, assemble them into a class booklet to be enjoyed by all.

Front

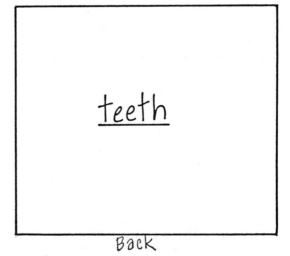

Back

REPRODUCIBLE ACTIVITY PAGE (GRADES 2–6)

Answer Key: Sample answers follow, but any answer that can be backed by logical reasoning should be accepted. (1) eye; (2) hands, face; (3) neck; (4) head; (5) tongue, eyes, heel, toe; (6) legs, feet, seat, back, arms; (7) teeth; (8) mouth, neck; (9) neck, shoulders; (10) body; (11) skin.

OBJECTS WITH BODY PARTS

Some objects have parts with names that are the same as names of parts of our bodies. For example, we have teeth, and a zipper has teeth.

Read the words below and think about what body part or parts each object has. Use the words in the *WORD BANK* to help you fill in as many blanks as you can.

Do you know what body parts I have?

WORD BANK			
head	teeth	seat	skin
heel	tongue	legs	arms
eye or eyes	feet	hands	neck
face	mouth	toe	
shoulders	body	back	

WHAT BODY PARTS DO THESE OBJECTS HAVE?

1. needle _____

2. clock _____ , _____

3. bottle _____

4. pin _____

5. shoe _____ , _____ , _____ , _____

6. chair _____ , _____ , _____ , _____ , _____

7. saw _____

8. jar _____ , _____

9. shirt _____ , _____

10. car _____

11. peach _____

24   HOW COULD YOU USE A _____?

Materials needed:

unlined paper (6″ x 9″ for class book)
pencil
Optional: crayons

☒ reproducible page
☒ total group activity
☒ individual activity
☐ partner activity

INDIVIDUAL ACTIVITY

The student thinks of an item that can be used in a variety of ways. For example, a brick could be used as a bookend, as a paperweight, as a doorstop, as a weight to hold strings attached to helium balloons...

On the front side of a piece of 6″ x 9″ paper, the student draws a picture of the object and writes the question, "How many ways could you use a _____?" At least two answers are written on the back of the paper.

Front   **Back**

When a sufficient number of papers have been collected, assemble them into a booklet for individual or whole-class use. However, before the booklet is used in the classroom, students should decide whether additional answers are to be written in the booklet, or whether they should be shared verbally, but not written. (Some students are bothered by others writing on *their* work, so it is important that ground rules are established.)

TOTAL GROUP ADAPTATION (GRADES 3–6)

Materials needed:

"How Could You Use a _____?" reproducible activity page, one for each student
pencils

Distribute the reproducible page and briefly discuss its format. After students have had time to complete the page, have them share their answers. Call attention to the diversity of their thinking and encourage them to share additional ideas that were generated by the discussion.

REPRODUCIBLE ACTIVITY PAGE (GRADES 3–6)

Students are asked to write *at least two ways* each object could be used. However, extra space has been provided for those who have additional ideas.

Answer Key: Sample answers follow, but any answer that can be backed by logical reasoning should be accepted. (1) *wastebasket*: paint face and add hair, attach a steering wheel and use as a pretend car, fill with water and use as a fishbowl, use as a target to toss things into; (2) *broom*: make it into a pretend horse, use it as the center pole for a tent, pretend it's a microphone, add wings and pretend it is an airplane; (3) *ladder*: lay it flat and hop between the rungs, turn it on its side and use it as a "net" for a modified game of tennis, use it as a hopscotch court; (4) *old parachute*: make a ghost costume out of it, put it over a table and build a "fort," get friends to pull on the edges with you and bounce balls on it, use as a shade covering; (5) *buttons*: use as markers for a board game, use as wheels on miniature toys, use for eyes on a doll, make designs with them; (6) *can*: use as a pencil holder, as a tower on a castle, as a cookie cutter, decorate and use as a flower container.

HOW COULD YOU USE A _____?

Often there are unusual ways an object could be used. For instance, a brick could be used to hold strings that were attached to helium balloons, or it could be used as a bookend.

List *at least two* unusual ways to use each of the following objects.

wastebasket	old parachute
1. _____	1. _____
2. _____	2. _____
3. _____	3. _____
4. _____	4. _____
broom	buttons
1. _____	1. _____
2. _____	2. _____
3. _____	3. _____
4. _____	4. _____
ladder	can
1. _____	1. _____
2. _____	2. _____
3. _____	3. _____
4. _____	4. _____

25 UNSUSPECTED SIMILARITIES

Materials needed:

lined paper (6″ x 9″ for class book)
pencil

☒ reproducible page
☒ total group activity
☒ individual activity
☐ partner activity

INDIVIDUAL ACTIVITY

The student thinks of two items that are alike in two or more ways. Encourage them to think beyond the obvious similarities and to look for interrelationships that may never have occurred to them before. For example, a window and a pair of eyeglasses: if they are dirty it is difficult to see clearly, both can be tinted, people look through both of them...

On the front side of a piece of 6″ x 9″ paper, the student writes the question: How are a _____ and a _____ alike? On the back of the paper, the student writes at least two ways the items are similar.

How are a window
and a pair of eye-
glasses alike?

≡ Front ≡

1. Both can be tinted.
2. If they are dirty
it's hard to see
through them.

≡ Back ≡

When a sufficient number of papers have been collected, assemble them into a booklet for individual or whole-class use. However, before the booklet is used in the classroom, students should decide whether additional answers are to be written in the booklet or whether they should be shared verbally, but not written. (Some students are bothered by others writing on *their* work, so it's important that ground rules are established.)

TOTAL GROUP ADAPTATION (GRADES 3–6)

Materials needed:

"Unsuspected Similarities" reproducible activity page, one for each student
pencils

Distribute the reproducible page and briefly discuss its format. After students have had time to complete the page, have them share their answers. Discuss the diversity of their thinking and have them share additional ideas that occur to them as they listen to the thoughts of others.

REPRODUCIBLE ACTIVITY PAGE (GRADES 3–6)

Students are asked to write *at least two ways* in which the pairs of words are alike. However, an extra line has been provided for those who perceive an additional similarity.

Answer Key: Sample answers follow, but any answer that can be backed by logical reasoning should be accepted. (1) *fly swatter/bat*: used to strike at objects, are held in the hand, takes practice to have success with them; (2) *telescope/eye*: used for seeing objects, are able to see objects at a distance, both require light; (3) *dog/human*: have ways of showing happiness, provide friendship, get upset if scolded; (4) *skateboard/bicycle*: are used to move a person from one place to another, require practice to learn the necessary skills, get their energy from a human.

NAME _____

UNSUSPECTED SIMILARITIES

It's fun to think about how two objects are alike.
It gets even more interesting when the objects
are ones that you have never compared before.
For example, how are eyeglasses and a window
alike? (Two possible answers: If they are
dirty it is hard to see through them.
Both of them can be tinted.)

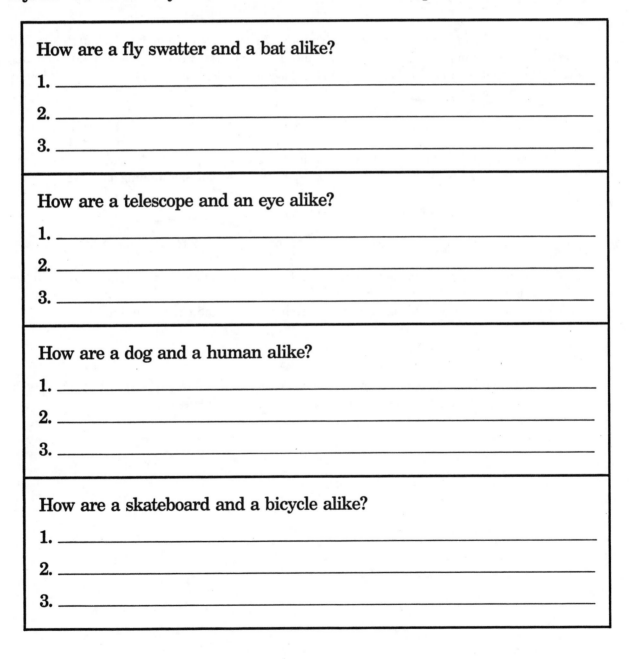

List *at least* two ways the following pairs of
objects are alike. Try to think of some unusual comparisons.

How are a fly swatter and a bat alike?

1. _____

2. _____

3. _____

How are a telescope and an eye alike?

1. _____

2. _____

3. _____

How are a dog and a human alike?

1. _____

2. _____

3. _____

How are a skateboard and a bicycle alike?

1. _____

2. _____

3. _____

26 NUMBER LINE JUMP

Materials needed:

chalk
chalkboard

☐ reproducible page
☒ total group activity
☐ individual activity
☐ partner activity

TOTAL GROUP ACTIVITY

On the chalkboard, write a number line, counting by ones from zero to fifteen. Tell the students to pretend a frog is jumping along the number line. Draw a series of curving lines to indicate where the frog lands on its first two or three jumps. Then have the students determine where it will land on each succeeding jump.

Continue using the same number line but have the frog jump by 2s, 4s, and 5s. Then draw a number line that counts by 2s (2, 4, 6...), 3s, or 4s, and continue questioning as above.

Write the following number pattern on the board.

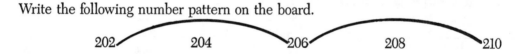

Without writing any additional numerals, ask the students to determine where the frog will land on its next jump, on the following jump, etc.

Write a number line with dots underneath each numeral, and extend the line of dots.

Put a question mark above one of the dots and ask what numeral would be at that position. As the numeral is filled in, erase the question mark and move it to a different dot.

27 PATTERN DETECTIVE

Materials needed:

chalk
chalkboard

☒ reproducible page
☒ total group activity
☐ individual activity
☐ partner activity

TOTAL GROUP ACTIVITY

Write the beginning of a pattern on the board.

$$19, \quad 17, \quad 15, \underline{\quad}, \underline{\quad}, \underline{\quad},$$

Call on students to name each suceeding number. If students are unsure of the pattern, remind them to look at the first two numerals and determine what happened between them. They should ask themselves questions, for example, "Is the second number larger or smaller? How much larger or smaller? Which math operation was used to make it larger or smaller?" Write the resulting answer between each pair of numerals. Continue until the pattern emerges. For example:

$$19, \overset{-2}{\quad} 17, \overset{-2}{\quad} 15, \underline{\quad}, \underline{\quad}, \underline{\quad},$$

Continue in the same manner using other patterns. Use operations and patterns that provide a challenge for your students.

Discover the Pattern

(1) $11, \overset{+3}{\quad} 14, \overset{+3}{\quad} 17, \quad \underline{\quad}, \quad \underline{\quad}, \quad \underline{\quad},$

(2) $30, \overset{-5}{\quad} 25, \overset{-5}{\quad} 20, \quad \underline{\quad}, \quad \underline{\quad}, \quad \underline{\quad},$

(3) $13, \overset{+4}{\quad} 17, \overset{+4}{\quad} 21, \quad \underline{\quad}, \quad \underline{\quad}, \quad \underline{\quad},$

(4) $1, \overset{\times 3}{\quad} 3, \overset{\times 3}{\quad} 9, \overset{\times 3}{\quad} 27, \quad \underline{\quad}, \quad \underline{\quad}, \quad \underline{\quad},$

(5) $1, \overset{+3}{\quad} 4, \overset{-1}{\quad} 3, \overset{+3}{\quad} 6, \overset{-1}{\quad} 5, \quad \underline{\quad}, \quad \underline{\quad}, \quad \underline{\quad},$

(6) $12, \overset{+5}{\quad} 17, \overset{-3}{\quad} 14, \overset{+5}{\quad} 19, \overset{-3}{\quad} 16, \quad \underline{\quad}, \quad \underline{\quad}, \quad \underline{\quad},$

(7) $2, \overset{\times 6}{\quad} 12, \overset{\div 3}{\quad} 4, \overset{\times 6}{\quad} 24, \overset{\div 3}{\quad} 8, \quad \underline{\quad}, \quad \underline{\quad}, \quad \underline{\quad},$

REPRODUCIBLE ACTIVITY PAGE (GRADES 2–4)

Answer Key:

A. (+4) 21, 25, 29, 33

B. (−2) 9, 7, 5, 3

C. (+4, −2) 16, 20, 18, 22

D. (−3) 9, 6, 3, 0

E. (+3, −1) 8, 11, 10, 13

F. (+3) 17, 20, 23, 26

G. (+1, +2) 7, 8, 10, 11

H. (+1, −2) 11, 12, 10, 11

NAME_____

PATTERN DETECTIVE

Look at the numbers below. Each number that is in a box shows what happened between the two numbers that are just below that box. Look for a pattern. Then continue the pattern.

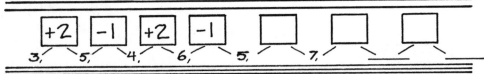

Finish the patterns below.

Ask yourself: Is the second number larger or smaller?

How much larger or smaller?

Was a plus sign or a minus sign used to make the number larger or smaller?

What is the pattern?

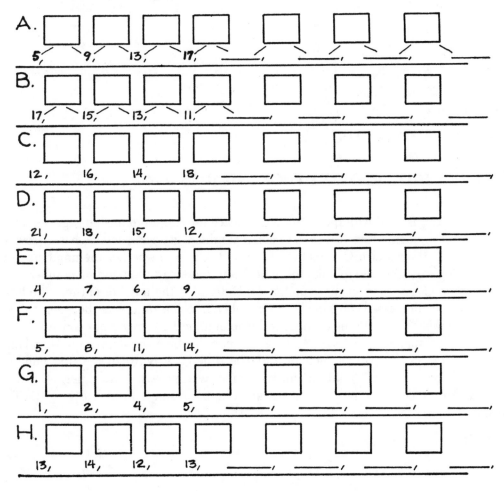

28 RHYTHM WITH NUMBERS

Materials needed:

☒ reproducible page
☒ total group activity
☐ individual activity
☐ partner activity

TOTAL GROUP ACTIVITY

Say one of the following number patterns aloud. For example; "2, 5, 8, 11." As students discover the pattern, ask them to join in and say the numbers with you. Use a rhythmic pointing signal to indicate when each number should be said and two hands held upright as a stopping signal. Keep going until all students have joined in, then begin a new pattern.

Sample Patterns

4, 7, 10, 13, 16, 19, ... (+3)
3, 5, 7, 9, 11, 13, ... (+2)
43, 45, 47, 49, 51, 53, ... (+2)
56, 53, 50, 47, 44, 41, ... (−3)
74, 72, 70, 68, 66, ... (−2)
156, 159, 162, 165, 168, ... (+3)
193, 191, 189, 187, 185, ... (−2)
172, 176, 180, 184, 188, 192, ... (+4)

REPRODUCIBLE ACTIVITY PAGE (GRADES 4–6)

If this activity is used with the entire class, distribute the reproducible page and briefly discuss its format. After students have had time to complete the page, ask if anyone has discovered a way to quickly discover the pattern. One method follows: (1) Observe whether the numbers in the pattern increase or decrease. (2) Find the difference between the starting and ending number by subtracting the larger number from the smaller number. (3) Determine the number of times the initial number was increased or decreased. (4) Divide this number into the difference between the starting and ending number. (5) The resulting number is the amount of the increase or decrease that was used in the pattern. For example, the first pattern on the reproducible page starts with 34 and ends with 54. (1) The numbers in the pattern increase. (2) The difference between the first number and final number is 20 (54 − 34 = 20). (3) The initial number was increased five times. (4) If five is divided into the difference between the first and last number, the result is 4 (20 ÷ 5 = 4). (5) Therefore the pattern is +4.

Discuss approaches that the students used to find the patterns. Working as a total group, apply these strategies to a variety of number patterns. (The patterns in the total group activity, "Rhythm with Numbers," can be used for this purpose.)

Answer Key:
A. 34, 38, 42, 46, 50, 54, (+4)
B. 87, 84, 81, 78, 75, 72, (−3)
C. 191, 193, 195, 197, 199, 201, (+2)
D. 104, 109, 114, 119, 124, 129, (+5)
E. 894, 893, 892, 891, 890, 889, (−1)

F. 759, 755, 751, 747, 743, 739, (−4)
G. 900, 895, 890, 885, 880, 875, (−5)
H. 531, 534, 537, 540, 543, 546, (+3)
I. 679, 677, 675, 673, 671, 669, (−2)

RHYTHM WITH NUMBERS

Look at the following numbers:
22, 25, 28, 31, 34, 37

The pattern starts at 22 and ends at 37. Three has been added to each number. Therefore the pattern is +3.

In the following patterns, you are given the beginning number and the ending number. Find the pattern and fill in the missing numbers. (*Hint:* The numbers never go up or down by more than 5.) CAN YOU FIND A WAY TO QUICKLY DISCOVER THE PATTERN?

©1989 by The Center for Applied Research in Education

A. 34, ——, ——, ——, ——, 54   What was the pattern? ——

B. 87, ——, ——, ——, ——, 72   What was the pattern? ——

C. 191, ——, ——, ——, ——, 201   What was the pattern? ——

D. 104, ——, ——, ——, ——, 129   What was the pattern? ——

E. 894, ——, ——, ——, ——, 889   What was the pattern? ——

F. 759, ——, ——, ——, ——, 739   What was the pattern? ——

G. 900, ——, ——, ——, ——, 875   What was the pattern? ——

H. 531, ——, ——, ——, ——, 546   What was the pattern? ——

I. 679, ——, ——, ——, ——, 669   What was the pattern? ——

29   HIDE AND SEEK

Materials needed:

chalkboard
chalk
chalk eraser
½ sheet of lined paper for each student
pencil for each student

☒ reproducible page
☒ total group activity
☐ individual activity
☐ partner activity

TOTAL GROUP ACTIVITY

Write a numeral on the board and underline one of its digits.

Example: 672.

Ask what the underlined numeral stands for (7 tens). Then ask what its value is in ones (70). Erase the line and underline a different digit. Use the same process with other numerals.

When students seems confident, hand out half sheets of lined paper. Have students write the numbers you dictate, skipping a line between each. Example: 14, 311, 39, 74, 714, 237, 63, 543, 639.

Ask the students to circle all 4s that are in the ones column, and to put a square around all 3s in the tens place.

Have them turn their papers over. Select two new categories, such as 7s in the ones column and 9s in the tens place. Dictate a new series of numbers, making certain that there are several numerals in each of the categories selected.

This activity can be extended by having students write the value in ones, next to each circled numeral.

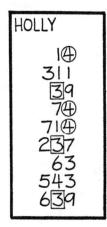

REPRODUCIBLE ACTIVITY PAGE (GRADES 1–2)

If this activity is used with the entire class, distribute the reproducible page and briefly discuss its format. Call particular attention to the directions at the bottom of the page and explain that by following these directions *many different* designs can be made. Stress that there is no one "right" design.

Students will enjoy having their completed pages displayed so they can compare the various designs made by their classmates.

Answer Key: The students' designs will vary.

HIDE AND SEEK

Make a red circle around each 3 that is in the ones column.

Make a blue box around each 7 that is in the tens column.

Make a green "X" on each 9 that is in the hundreds column.

933	789	397	943
955	573	773	989
997	873	673	964
993	797	589	963

Take your green crayon. Make a design by connecting green Xs.

Take your blue crayon. Make a design by connecting blue boxes.

Take your red crayon. Make a design by connecting red circles.

30 LITTLE DIFFERENCES ARE NOT SO LITTLE

Materials needed:

chalkboard
chalk

☒ reproducible page
☒ total group activity
☐ individual activity
☐ partner activity

TOTAL GROUP ACTIVITY

For students in grades 1–3, write five similar numerals on the chalkboard along with the following diagrams.

Tell students that you will read one of the numbers. They should find the numeral on the chalkboard and then look at the "signal" above the numeral (folded hands, hands on head, hands extended to sides, hands behind back, or one finger wiggling).

Remind them to think before signaling. To provide them thinking time, after you read a word hold up your opened hand and silently count to five. They should respond when you close your fist. If students look around to see what others have done, before giving their own hand signal, change the directions to, "Close eyes." (pause) "Show me...Open eyes."

Identify the correct answer. Then point to one of the incorrect numerals and ask a student why he or she did not select that one. This provides a good opportunity for students to use language that relates to place value.

Say one of the other numbers and continue as above. Follow the same procedure until all the numerals are identified. Then write a new series of numerals that are quite similar and continue in the same manner.

For upper grade students, follow the above procedure, incorporating decimal points in the numerals. For example:

108.6   10.86   1.086   10.086

REPRODUCIBLE ACTIVITY PAGE (GRADES 2–4)

Answer Key: A. 3855; B. 2004; C. 6992; D. 1330; E. 49; F. 717; G. 8366; H. 5676.

LITTLE DIFFERENCES ARE NOT SO LITTLE

Find the answer for each number riddle.

Make an "X" on all numbers that do not go with the clue.

EXAMPLE:	CLUE: I have a zero in the tens place.			
	213	2003	23	2040

An "X" would be made on the numbers 213, 23, and 2040 since they do not have a zero in the tens place. After you have worked all the clues for each riddle, there should be only one number left.

©1989 by The Center for Applied Research in Education

A. 38   3855   358   3538   3585

I have a 5 in the ones place.

I am greater than 300.

I have an 8 in the hundreds place.

B. 204   2004   24   2400   2040

I have a 4 in the ones place.

There is a zero somewhere in my number.

I am greater than 800.

C. 6992   6299   662   6929   92

I have a 2 in the ones place.

I am greater than 100.

The number in the tens place = 90.

D. 1330   33   1033   1303   130

There is a zero somewhere in my number.

The number in the tens place = 30.

I am greater than 1300.

E. 49   4249   449   4942   4292

The number in the tens place = 40.

I have a 9 in the ones place.

I am less than 400.

F. 5171   717   51   5711   5717

The number in the hundreds place = 700.

I have a 7 in the ones place.

I am less than 770.

G. 8663   8536   383   836   8366

I am less than 8600.

I am greater than 800.

I have a 3 in the hundreds place.

H. 567   5677   57   5786   5676

I am greater than 5,000.

The number in the hundreds place = 600.

I have a 6 in the ones place.

31 WHAT'S IN BETWEEN?

Materials needed:

☒ reproducible page
☒ total group activity
☐ individual activity
☐ partner activity

TOTAL GROUP ACTIVITY

Ask students to name the odd numbers or the even numbers greater than one number and less than another number that you name. For example, name all of the even numbers that are greater than 35 but less than 59 (36, 38, 40, 42, 44, 46, 48, 50, 52, 54, 56, 58).

Follow Up: The activity can be extended by repeating it on a different day and having the students write their answers on paper.

What's in Between These?

1. Odd numbers that are greater than 47 but less than 68
   (49, 51, 53, 55, 57, 59, 61, 63, 65, 67)

2. Even numbers that are greater than 67 but less than 91
   (68, 70, 72, 74, 76, 78, 80, 82, 84, 86, 88, 90)

3. Odd numbers that are greater than 30 but less than 52
   (31, 33, 35, 37, 39, 41, 43, 45, 47, 49, 51)

4. Even numbers that are greater than 55 but less than 79
   (56, 58, 60, 62, 64, 66, 68, 70, 72, 74, 76, 78)

5. Odd numbers that are greater than 74 but less than 95
   (75, 77, 79, 81, 83, 85, 87, 89, 91, 93)

6. Even numbers that are greater than 82 but less than 98
   (84, 86, 88, 90, 92, 94, 96)

7. Odd numbers that are greater than 156 but less than 175
   (157, 159, 161, 163, 165, 167, 169, 171, 173)

8. Even numbers that are greater than 278 but less than 298
   (280, 282, 284, 286, 288, 290, 292, 294, 296)

REPRODUCIBLE ACTIVITY PAGE (GRADES 2–3)

Answer Key:

(1) 79, 81, 83, 85, 87, 89, 91, 93, 95, 97
(2) 48, 50, 52, 54, 56, 58, 60, 62, 64
(3) 33, 35, 37, 39, 41, 43, 45, 47, 49, 51
(4) 66, 68, 70, 72, 74, 76, 78, 80, 82

(5) 75, 77, 79, 81, 83, 85, 87, 89, 91, 93
(6) 54, 56, 58, 60, 62, 64, 66
(7) 177, 179, 181, 183, 185, 187, 189, 191, 193
(8) 260, 262, 264, 266, 268, 270, 272, 274, 276

WHAT'S IN BETWEEN?

Write the answers in the blanks.

1. Odd numbers that are greater than 77 but less than 98

_____ , _____ , _____ , _____ , _____ , _____ , _____ , _____ , _____ , _____

2. Even numbers that are greater than 47 but less than 65

_____ , _____ , _____ , _____ , _____ , _____ , _____ , _____ , _____

3. Odd numbers that are greater than 32 but less than 52

_____ , _____ , _____ , _____ , _____ , _____ , _____ , _____ , _____ , _____

4. Even numbers that are greater than 65 but less than 83

_____ , _____ , _____ , _____ , _____ , _____ , _____ , _____ , _____

5. Odd numbers that are greater than 74 but less than 95

_____ , _____ , _____ , _____ , _____ , _____ , _____ , _____ , _____ , _____

6. Even numbers that are greater than 52 but less than 68

_____ , _____ , _____ , _____ , _____ , _____ , _____

7. Odd numbers that are greater than 176 but less than 195

_____ , _____ , _____ , _____ , _____ , _____ , _____ , _____ , _____

8. Even numbers that are greater than 258 but less than 278

_____ , _____ , _____ , _____ , _____ , _____ , _____ , _____ , _____

32   CALENDAR PUZZLES

Materials needed:

chalkboard
chalk
eraser
calendar drawn on chalkboard
or
calendar posted in room

☒ reproducible page
☒ total group activity
☐ individual activity
☐ partner activity

TOTAL GROUP ACTIVITY

Draw a calendar of the current month on the chalkboard or post a calendar where all students can see it. Randomly call on students to answer the following questions. (This activity can be repeated throughout the year.)

Calendar Puzzles

1. What *day* is the 12th of this month?—What is the date one week earlier?—One week later?
2. Name the dates that fall on *all* Tuesdays this month.
3. How many days have passed since the _____ of this month?
4. How many Wednesdays are there between the 10th and the 29th of this month?
5. What is today's date? If you were going to a party on the _____, how many days would you have to wait?
6. How many Fridays are there this month?—How many of these dates are even numbers?
7. What date is the third Thursday this month?—What is the date two weeks earlier?
8. Which week has the fewest days?
9. Can you find two dates that you can add together to get a sum of 46?
10. Can you find a date that when subtracted from another date leaves 13?

REPRODUCIBLE ACTIVITY PAGE (GRADES 2–3)

Answer Key: (1) Sat.; March 31; (2) the first week; (3) 4; (4) 5, 3; (5) March 15, March 1; (6) 16; (7) Answers will vary; (8) Student's initials should be written on the calendar.

CALENDAR PUZZLES

Use the calendar below to answer the questions.

MARCH						
Sun.	Mon.	Tues.	Wed.	Thurs.	Fri.	Sat.
				1	2	3
4	5	6	7	8	9	10
11	12	13	14	15	16	17
18	19	20	21	22	23	24
25	26	27	28	29	30	31

1. What *day* is the 17th of March? _____

   What is the *date* two weeks later? _____

2. Which week has the fewest days? _____

3. How many Wednesdays are there between the 6th and the 29th of this month? _____

4. How many Fridays are there this month? _____ How many of these dates are even numbers? _____

5. What *date* is the third Thursday? _____ What is the date two weeks earlier? _____

6. How many dates on the calendar are odd numbers? _____

7. Can you find two dates that you can add together to get a sum of 49? ☐ + ☐ = _____

8. Write your first and last initials by connecting numbers on the calendar. (See the example at the top of the page.)

33 GRAPH FAVORITES

Materials needed:

chalkboard
chalk
eraser

optional: one copy of the
  reproducible graph and
  a pencil for each student

☒ reproducible page
☒ total group activity
☐ individual activity
☐ partner activity

TOTAL GROUP ACTIVITY

Students enjoy making graphs that relate to their personal interests and then discussing and comparing the results. In this activity, the teacher announces a general topic that entails making choices. Students then make suggestions for the choices to be voted on. For example, if the topic were, "If you had a choice, what would you most like to do during summer vacation?" the students might suggest the following choices: camp with family, travel, visit relatives, fish, play baseball, swim, go away to camp, etc.

As each choice is given, it should be listed on the chalkboard. If students make more than six suggestions, explain that they will be making a graph that needs to be limited to six items. Therefore the top six choices need to be determined. Take a quick vote by having each student raise his or her hand to vote for one item listed on the chalkboard. Record the results and then erase all but the six most popular choices.

Have students vote once more, this time indicating their favorite of the six remaining items. Count the votes for each choice and once more record the information on the chalkboard. This information can then be plotted by coloring in squares or writing Xs in the squares of a graph drawn on the chalkboard. Or students may plot the information on their own graph. (Use the graph found on the reproducible activity page.)

When the graph is completed, encourage the students to interpret the information by asking questions such as, "Which item received the most votes? Least votes?" "Compare _____ and _____. How many more votes did _____ get?" "How many fewer votes did _____ get?" "Did any items receive the same number of votes?"

Topics for Graphing

1. If you had a choice, what animal would you choose as a pet?
2. If you had a choice, at which fast food restaurant would you want to eat?

3. Which form of transportation would be your favorite way to come to school, car, bus, bike, or on foot?

4. If you could choose one activity to do at home with your family, what would it be?

5. If you had a choice, what would you most like to do during summer vacation?

6. If you could meet one TV star, who would you choose?

7. If you could meet one sports star, who would it be?

8. If you could go to one professional sporting event, what would your choice be?

9. If you could own a car, which make would you choose?

10. If you could see one musical group in person, what would your choice be?

Favorite Vacation

	0	1	2	3	4	5	6	7	8	9	10
camp with family											
travel											
visit relatives											
fish											
play baseball											
swim											

Favorite Vacation

	camp with family	travel	visit relatives	fish	play base. ball	swim
10						
9						
8	X					
7	X				X	
6	X				X	
5	X		X		X	X
4	X		X		X	X
3	X		X	X	X	X
2	X	X	X	X	X	X
1	X	X	X	X	X	X
0						

REPRODUCIBLE ACTIVITY PAGE (GRADES 1–6)

Follow the total group activity directions. The pertinent information should be written on the chalkboard so students can refer to it as needed. When the students have completed their graphs, the results should be discussed and compared.

Answer Key: Answers will vary.

8 - camp with family
2 - travel
5 - visit relatives
3 - fish
7 - play baseball
5 - swim

NAME _____

GRAPH FAVORITES

Write the title of the graph on the line below.

Write the choices on lines A through F.

Fill in the graph to show how your class voted.

_____ Title

	0	1	2	3	4	5	6	7	8	9	10	11	12	13	14	15	16	17	18	19	20
A.																					
B.																					
C.																					
D.																					
E.																					
F.																					

Fill in choices.

34   COORDINATE GHOST

Materials needed:

chalkboard
chalk
eraser

☒ reproducible page
☒ total group activity
☐ individual activity
☐ partner activity

TOTAL GROUP ACTIVITY

Draw a grid (five lines down, five lines across) on the chalkboard. Omitting the letter "z," write a letter of the alphabet slightly to the side of each intersection. Number horizontal lines and vertical lines from 0 to 4. Explain the numbering and lettering system, and point out that the letters are slightly to the side of the intersections so that students can easily see them.

	0	1	2	3	4
4	N	H	Q	L	F
3	C	P	D	Z	T
2	R	M	U	B	J
1	W	A	O	S	V
0	I	Y	G	K	E

Remind students that in grids, the horizontal line (generally the bottom line) is said first, followed by the vertical line. ("Walk to the mountain and then climb it.") Illustrate this as follows.

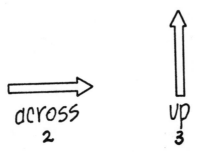

across
2

up
3

Then say, "I'm thinking of a letter. It is located at the intersection of 2 and 3. What is my letter?" (D). As students answer, erase the numerals and write a new pair under the words "across" and "up."

When the students can easily locate letters by using coordinates, divide the class into two teams and establish the order in which you will call on students. The first player on Team A selects a letter of the alphabet and names its corresponding coordinates. On the chalkboard, write the letter that is found at the specified intersection.

The first student on Team B thinks of a word that begins with that letter and says the coordinates for the second letter of the word. (Proper names, foreign words, and abbreviations may not be used.) Teams continue to alternate giving coordinates, trying *not* to be the one who completes a word that is four or more letters in length.

Words of one, two, or three letters do not count against a team. However, the first time a team gives a letter that completes a word of four or more letters, they receive a "G," and a new round is begun. The next time they complete a word, they receive an "H," etc., until the word "GHOST" is spelled. The first team with "GHOST" loses the game.

If the next player on the opposing team thinks the last letter is not part of a real word, the players says, "I challenge." If the previous player cannot give a real word, or misspells the intended word, his or her team loses the round and receives the next letter in "GHOST." However, if the player *can* give an appropriate word, the challenger loses the round and is "awarded" the letter.

When coordinates are given that result in a different letter than the one the student intended, the "incorrect letter" is the one that is written on the board. This encourages students to check carefully before announcing their choice of coordinates.

REPRODUCIBLE ACTIVITY PAGE (GRADES 3–6)

Answer Key: MARY HAD A LITTLE DOG,
WHO BARKED AT EVERY FLEA.
AND EVERY TIME THAT MARY SNEEZED,
THE DOG JUMPED ON HER KNEE.

NAME _____

COORDINATE RHYME

4	N	H	Q	L	F
3	C	P	D	Z	T
2	R	M	U	B	J
1	W	A	O	S	V
0	I	Y	G	K	E
	0	1	2	3	4

Look at the grid below. A letter of the alphabet is written at each point where two lines cross. To use the grid, go *across* then *up*. For example, the numbers 4, 3 mean go across the numbers at the bottom of the grid until you reach 4 and then go straight up until you are opposite the 3. The letter at that point is T.

Use the grid to discover each letter in the following riddle.

1,2   1,1 0,2 1,0   1,4 1,1 2,3   1,1   3,4 0,0 4,3 4,3 3,4 4,0   2,3 2,1 2,0

0,1   1,4 2,1   3,2 1,1 0,2 3,0 .   4,1 4,0 1,1   4,0 0,2 1,0   1,1 4,3

4,4 3,4 4,0 1,1

1,1   0,4 2,3   4,0   0,0 1,2 4,0   0,2 4,0 4,3   4,3 1,1 4,3   4,3 1,4 4,3

1,2   1,1 0,2 1,0   1,0 0,2 0,2   3,1 0,4 4,0   3,1 1,4 0,4   4,0 4,0 4,0   1,2 1,3 1,2   4,0 2,3 4,3   4,3 1,1 4,3

4,3   1,4 4,0   2,3 2,1 4,2 2,2 1,2   4,0 1,3 4,0   2,1 4,0 2,3   1,4 2,1 0,4   1,1 4,3   2,1 0,4

3,0   0,4 4,0 4,0   0,2

35 I'M HIDING

Materials needed:

chalkboard
chalk
eraser

☒ reproducible page
☒ total group activity
☐ individual activity
☒ partner activity

TOTAL GROUP ACTIVITY

Draw a 12-square by 12-square grid on the chalkboard and number each line. (See example below.) To the side draw a compass rose. Secretly write a set of coordinates on the chalkboard where it can't be seen or on a piece of paper, with numerals large enough to show students later.

Tell the class there is an "invisible X" hidden somewhere on the grid. You have written its location on a piece of paper (or on the chalkboard), and they are to try to find it. They should indicate each of their guesses by giving the coordinates for that position. You in turn will indicate what direction they need to go in order to find it.

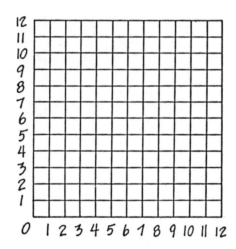
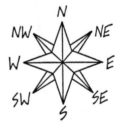

Remind them, when giving coordinates, to say the horizontal axis first, then the vertical axis. Give a few examples before beginning. Say, "If the 'X' were at the coordinates 4, 5 (point to the location), and someone guessed 7, 9 (again indicate the position), in what direction does the person need to go?" (Southwest) Continue in this manner until students understand the concept.

Then have them try to find the "invisible X." As each guess is made, write the coordinates and your direction clue on the chalkboard, so students can refer to the information as needed.

Guess	Clue
3, 4	NW
5, 8	S

The person who locates the "X" can become the leader for the next round.

PARTNER ADAPTATION (GRADES 4–6)

Materials needed:
"I'm Hiding" reproducible activity page
   (one copy for partners to share)
pencil
lined paper, one piece for each player

Partners follow the directions on the previous page. Player One secretly writes the coordinates of the "invisible X" on lined paper. Player Two guesses the location by writing the coordinates for that position. Player One writes the direction in which Player Two needs to go in order to find the hidden "X" (N, NW, NE, etc.). When the "X" is located, the players reverse roles.

REPRODUCIBLE ACTIVITY PAGE (GRADES 4–6)

Provide lined paper for students to use as they work this activity page.

Answer Key: Answers will vary.

I'M HIDING

Player One chooses a position on the grid for the location of an "invisible X" then secretly writes the coordinates for that location.

Player Two guesses where the hidden "X" is and writes the coordinates for that position on a piece of paper.

On the same paper, Player One writes the direction in which Player Two needs to go in order to find the hidden "X." For example, Player One might write "NE," telling Player Two to guess coordinates that are to the northeast.

Play continues until Player One finds the "X." Then players change roles.

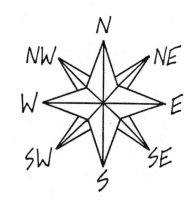

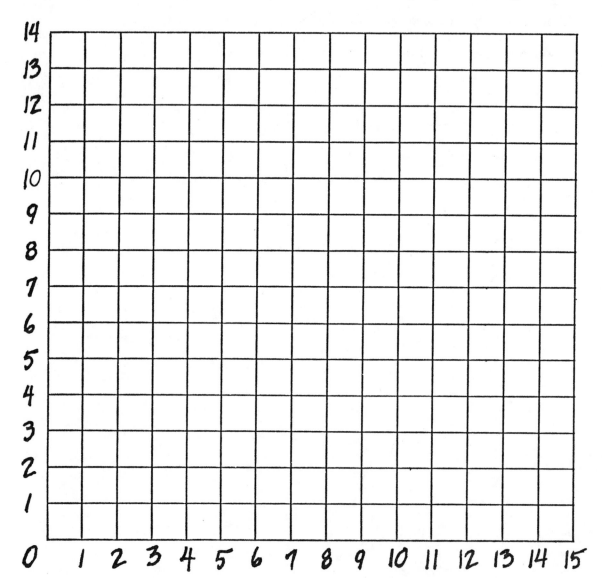

©1989 by The Center for Applied Research in Education

36   DIRECTIONS FROM A CLOCK!

Materials needed:

chalkboard
chalk
eraser

☒ reproducible page
☒ total group activity
☐ individual activity
☐ partner activity

TOTAL GROUP ACTIVITY

Draw the following diagram on the chalkboard and explain that directions are often given in relationship to the numbers on the face of a clock. For example, if someone said, "Look at that snow capped mountain at three o'clock," it would mean that the mountain was directly to your right. If the person had wanted you to look directly to your left, he or she would have said, "The mountain is at nine o'clock."

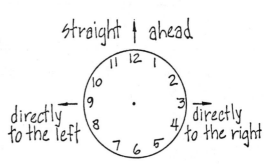

Explain that regardless of what direction a person is facing, twelve o'clock is always straight ahead, and the other clock directions relate to the person's current position.

Have the students determine the direction that would be indicated by ten o'clock, eleven o'clock, twelve o'clock, one o'clock, and two o'clock. Then have them face in the *opposite direction*. Ask, "Where is twelve o'clock now? Three o'clock? Nine o'clock?" and so forth.

When students are secure with this concept, have them take turns, giving two clues about an object in the room. One clue should be given in relationship to a clock face. The other clue should relate to one of the attributes of the object: size, color, shape, etc. Example: "I'm thinking of a large object that is at eleven o'clock," or "I'm thinking of a red object at two o'clock."

Make certain students understand that the clock direction is given *in relationship to the position of the person saying the riddle.* Give the example of three o'clock. This is not the same for a person seated at the front of the room as it is for a person in the back of the room. Therefore they need to pretend that they are in the "riddle giver's" position and determine the clock position from that person's vantage point.

The person who correctly identifies the object may give the next clues or may choose someone to give the clues.

REPRODUCIBLE ACTIVITY PAGE (GRADES 4–5)

Answer Key: Check to see that the appropriate drawing appears at the proper time by the clock.

DIRECTIONS FROM A CLOCK!

People often give directions as if they were looking at the face of a clock. An object that is straight ahead is at twelve o'clock. If something is at three o'clock it is directly to the right.

Put your pencil on a number on the clock and draw a line toward the outside edge of the box, but leave a space for a picture. Do this for each number. Then read the directions and draw each object where it belongs.

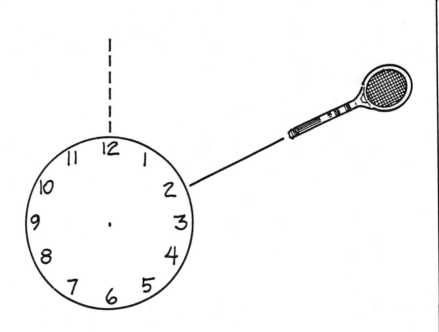

A. Draw a flag at twelve o'clock.	F. Draw a sun at eight o'clock.
B. Draw a glass at three o'clock.	G. A tennis racket has been drawn at two o'clock.
C. Draw a baseball bat at nine o'clock.	
D. Draw a pencil at one o'clock.	H. Draw a book at ten o'clock.
E. Draw a star at four o'clock.	I. Draw a flower at eleven o'clock.

37 WHAT'S THE TOTAL VALUE?

Materials needed:

chalk
chalkboard
eraser
lined paper for each student
pencil for each student

☒ reproducible page
☒ total group activity
☐ individual activity
☐ partner activity

TOTAL GROUP ACTIVITY

On the chalkboard write: penny, nickel, dime, quarter, half dollar, dollar. Write a numeral under several of the words, indicating the number of coins of that denomination.

penny	nickel	dime	quarter	half dollar	dollar
	1		1	1	

Ask students to determine the total value.

Example: I have one nickel, one quarter, and one half dollar. How much do I have?

Students may use mental math to determine the answer or use paper and pencil for making their calculations.

Variation

Tell students the number of coins you have and their total value. Students must determine how many coins of each denomination you have. Example: "I have 6 coins and their total value is 36¢. What are my coins?" (2 dimes, 3 nickels, 1 penny).

6 coins —— total value 36¢

Continue to present problems in either of the above formats until students can easily determine the answers. Then divide the class into two teams and number the players.

Alternate giving problems to the teams. Write the numerals under the words as each denomination is said. Or if the variation is used, write the number of coins and their total value. The player who is "up," gives the answer. Score is kept on the chalkboard and should be handled in the following manner:

1. Answer is correct. —**l point**
2. A mistake is made and the next person on the opposing team spots the mistake and gives the correct answer. —**Opposing team gets the point.**
3. A mistake is made and the next member of the opposing team does not spot the mistake. — **No points.**

The game ends when all students have had a turn, or at the end of a designated time period. The team with the most points is the winner.

Total Value and Number of Coins

	penny	nickel	dime	quarter	half dollar	dollar	TOTAL	TOTAL NUMBER OF COINS
1.	4	1	2				29¢	7
2.	6	2	1				26¢	9
3.	5	1	2				30¢	8
4.	2	2	2				32¢	6
5.	4	4	1				34¢	9
6.	7	2	2				37¢	11
7.	1	2	3				41¢	6
8.	8	2	2				38¢	12
9.	4	2	3				44¢	9
10.	5	1	3				40¢	9
11.	2	3	2				37¢	7
12.	8	4	2				48¢	14
13.	6	3	3				51¢	12
14.	7	2	4				57¢	13
15.	9	4	3				59¢	16
16.	3	5	2				48¢	10
17.	4	1	0	1			34¢	6
18.	3	0	1	1			38¢	5
19.	2	1	3	1			62¢	7

	penny	nickel	dime	quarter	half dollar	dollar	TOTAL	TOTAL NUMBER OF COINS
20.	0	2	4	1			75¢	7
21.	4	1	2	2			79¢	9
22.	9	0	4	2			99¢	15
23.	4	1	0	2	1		$1.09	8
24.	3	2	1	2	1		$1.23	9
25.	7	1	1	2	1		$1.22	12
26.	5	2	3	0	2		$1.45	12
27.	4	2	2	2	1		$1.34	11
28.	3	2	1	3	1		$1.48	10
29.	8	3	4	2	1		$1.63	18
30.	7	2	3	1	2		$1.72	15
31.	5	4	2	3	2	1	$3.20	17
32.	7	2	3	2	3	4	$6.47	21
33.	2	3	4	1	2	3	$4.82	15
34.	3	4	2	2	3	7	$9.43	21
35.	8	2	4	3	2	2	$4.33	21
36.	4	2	6	0	4	9	$11.74	25
37.	2	3	5	3	3	7	$9.92	23
38.	6	4	3	4	2	8	$10.56	27
39.	7	6	2	4	3	9	$12.07	31
40.	3	5	4	4	3	6	$9.18	25

REPRODUCIBLE ACTIVITY PAGE (GRADES 3–4)

Answer Key: (1) 2 pennies, 5 nickels, 2 dimes; (2) 2 pennies, 1 nickel, 3 dimes, 1 quarter; (3) 6 pennies, 3 nickels, 3 dimes; (4) 2 nickels, 4 dimes, 1 quarter; (5) 7 pennies, 2 nickels, 4 dimes; (6) 4 pennies, 1 nickel, 2 dimes, 2 quarters; (7) 7 pennies, 1 nickel, 1 dime, 2 quarters, 1 half dollar; (8) 3 pennies, 2 nickels, 1 dime, 3 quarters, 1 half dollar.

WHAT'S THE TOTAL VALUE?

Read the money riddles below. Write how many of each coin you would need in order to solve the riddles.

P = penny   N = nickel   D = dime   Q = quarter   HD = half dollar

1. I have 9 coins.

The total value is 47¢.

What are my coins?

___P, ___N, ___D, ___Q, ___HD

2. I have 7 coins.

The total value is 62¢.

What are my coins?

___P, ___N, ___D, ___Q, ___HD

3. I have 12 coins.

The total value is 51¢.

What are my coins?

___P, ___N, ___D, ___Q, ___HD

4. I have 7 coins.

The total value is 75¢.

What are my coins?

___P, ___N, ___D, ___Q, ___HD

5. I have 13 coins.

The total value is 57¢.

What are my coins?

___P, ___N, ___D, ___Q, ___HD

6. I have 9 coins.

The total value is 79¢.

What are my coins?

___P, ___N, ___D, ___Q, ___HD

7. I have 12 coins.

The total value is $1.22.

What are my coins?

___P, ___N, ___D, ___Q, ___HD

8. I have 10 coins.

The total value is $1.48.

What are my coins?

___P, ___N, ___D, ___Q, ___HD

38   ANALYZE THE ALPHABET

Materials needed:

chalkboard
chalk
eraser

☒ reproducible page
☒ total group activity
☐ individual activity
☐ partner activity

TOTAL GROUP ACTIVITY

Write *line segment* on the chalkboard and remind students that a line segment is a straight line that starts and stops at end points. Challenge students to analyze the capital letters of the alphabet and try to locate all the letters that are made *only* of line segments.

Write a capital A on the chalkboard and ask whether it fits the designated category. If they are unsure of the answer, write the first stroke and ask whether it is a line segment. Continue, writing one stroke at a time, until they identify the letter as being made completely of line segments. Then write "A" on the chalkboard under the heading.

Analyze several letters of the alphabet, recording their answers on the chalkboard. When they encounter letters that do not fit within the designated category, write them to the side in a "Discard Pile." (See illustration below.)

At this point, you may either give students the accompanying Reproducible Page to work independently, or the students may continue to work together analyzing the entire alphabet.

Line Segments	Discard
A	B
E	C
F	D
H	G
I	J
K	O
L	P
M	Q
N	R
T	S
V	U
W	
X	
Y	
Z	

REPRODUCIBLE ACTIVITY PAGE (GRADES 1–4)

Answer Key: *Line Segments:* A, E, F, H, I, K, L, M, N, T, V, W, X, Y, Z; *Discard:* B, C, D, G, J, O, P, Q, R, S, U.

Suggestion: If you do not have time to duplicate the reproducible page, as an alternative procedure have each student divide a paper in two columns and label them "Line Segment" and "Discard." Letters that are composed completely of line segments are written under the first heading. All other letters are written in the "discard" column.

ANALYZE THE ALPHABET

A line segment is a straight line that has beginning and end points.

In the box labeled "Letters," write the alphabet in capital letters. Then look at each letter. If it is made *only* of line segments, write it in the box labeled "Line Segments." If any part of the letter is not a line segment, write it in the box labeled "Discard."
When you are finished, you should have 15 letters in the "Line Segment" box and 11 letters in the "Discard" box.

Letters	Line Segments	Discard
A	A	B
B		

39   3-D INSIDE/OUTSIDE CHALLENGE

Materials needed:

chalkboard
chalk
eraser
½ sheet of paper for each student
pencil for each student

☒ reproducible page
☒ total group activity
☐ individual activity
☐ partner activity

TOTAL GROUP ACTIVITY

Draw overlapping three-dimensional shapes on the chalkboard like the ones shown here. Put dots, or a combination of dots and Xs inside the shapes. Then ask interpretive questions such as those in the following example:

1.   How many dots are in the cube? **(3)**
2.   How many dots are in both the cone and the cylinder? **(1)**
3.   How many X's are in both the cube and the cylinder? **(2)**
4.   How many dots are outside the cube? **(3)**
5.   How many Xs are in the cube, but not in the cylinder or cone? **(4)**

If students are not sure how an answer was derived, have one student come to the chalkboard and trace the designated shape(s) with a finger and then identify the number of dots or Xs within the specified area.

Once students understand the process, ask them to number a half sheet of paper from one to ten. Draw a new set of overlapping three-dimensional shapes on the chalkboard and ask similar questions, having the students record their answers on paper. Another sample is shown here.

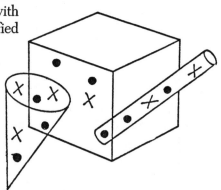

REPRODUCIBLE ACTIVITY PAGE (GRADES 3–6)

Answer Key: A: (1) 2   B: (1) 2   C: (1) 2   D: (1) 2
              (2) 3   (2) 4   (2) 1   (2) 1
              (3) 4   (3) 1   (3) 1   (3) 3
              (4) 1   (4) 3   (4) 0   (4) 1

3-D INSIDE/OUTSIDE CHALLENGE

Look at the drawings below. Read the directions and write your answers on the blanks. Watch out! These can be tricky!

A.

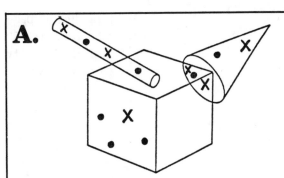

1. How many X's
   are in the cylinder? _____

2. How many X's
   are in the cone? _____

3. How many X's
   are outside the cylinder? _____

4. How many •'s
   are in both the cube
   and the cone? _____

B.

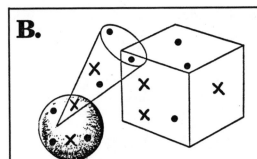

1. How many X's
   are in the cone? _____

2. How many •'s
   are in the cube? _____

3. How many X's are in both
   the cone and the sphere? _____

4. How many •'s
   are in the sphere? _____

C.

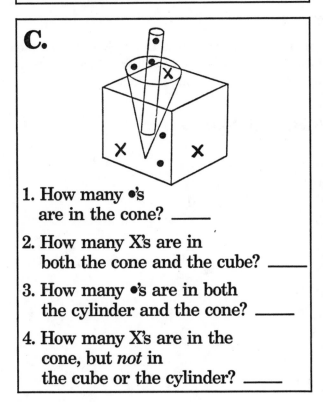

1. How many •'s
   are in the cone? _____

2. How many X's are in
   both the cone and the cube? _____

3. How many •'s are in both
   the cylinder and the cone? _____

4. How many X's are in the
   cone, but *not* in
   the cube or the cylinder? _____

D.

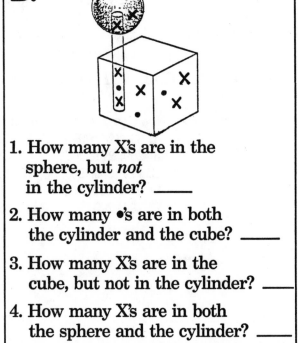

1. How many X's are in the
   sphere, but *not*
   in the cylinder? _____

2. How many •'s are in both
   the cylinder and the cube? _____

3. How many X's are in the
   cube, but not in the cylinder? _____

4. How many X's are in both
   the sphere and the cylinder? _____

40   COMPARING NUMBERS

Materials needed:

chalkboard
chalk
eraser

☒ reproducible page
☒ total group activity
☐ individual activity
☐ partner activity

TOTAL GROUP ACTIVITY

On the chalkboard write:

$$47 < 51$$

Discuss the symbol (less than) and ask students which numbers are greater than 47, but less than 51. Write the numerals on the chalkboard as they are named (**48, 49, 50**). Then ask which numbers are less than 73, but greater than 67. Write:

$$73 > 67$$

Discuss the symbol (greater than) and write the numerals as they are named (**72, 71, 70, 69, 68**).

Give several examples of both greater than and less than, using two-digit numbers, and then by three-digit numbers, until students understand the symbols.

To play the game, begin by writing on the chalkboard:

$$27 > ?$$

Tell the students that you are going to say numbers. If the numbers can replace the question mark, they are to stand. If not, they should remain seated. Say several numbers, then change the numeral on the chalkboard, vary the symbol, and continue in the same manner.

REPRODUCIBLE ACTIVITY PAGE (GRADES 2–3)

Answer Key: Numbers given are those that should be boxed.

A. 89, 126, 90	**F.** 229, 219	**K.** 173
B. 269, 271, 267	**G.** 107	**L.** 251
C. 199, 209, 205	**H.** 239	
D. 198, 239, 235	**I.** 170	
E. 294, 290	**J.** 161	

COMPARING NUMBERS

For each of the following problems, make a box around *all* numbers that can be written in place of the question mark.

A.

? > 85

89   126   79   90

B.

276 > ?

269   280   271   267

C.

? < 213

199   220   209   205

D.

? < 240

198   239   251   235

E.

289 < ?

287   294   199   290

F.

234 > ?

229   219   237   249

Here are some more number puzzles. Make a box around the correct answer.

G.

Which number is greater than 85, but less than 109?

119   107   111   113

H.

Which number is less than 243, but greater than 199?

247   189   245   239

I.

Which number is greater than 165, but less than 173?

182   175   170   159

J.

Which number is less than 179, but greater than 158?

182   149   161   155

K.

Which number is greater than 162, but less than 181?

L.

Which number is less than 274, but greater than 239?

41   ASK AND ANSWER

Materials needed:

chalkboard
chalk
eraser

☒ reproducible page
☒ total group activity
☐ individual activity
☐ partner activity

TOTAL GROUP ACTIVITY

Write four or five numerals on the chalkboard. Then ask questions that use the terms:

least
greatest
less than
greater than
greater than _____ and less than _____
less than _____ and greater than _____

Example: 42   57   25   64   48

1.   Which number is least? (**25**)
2.   Which is greatest? (**64**)
3.   Which numbers are less than 57? (**25, 42, and 48**)
4.   Which numbers are greater than 48? (**57 and 64**)
5.   Which number is greater than 42 and less than 57? (**48**)
6.   Which number is less than 64 and greater than 48? (**57**)

When students are acquainted with these questions, write the above terms on the board. Have them take turns asking questions and calling on other students. The person who gives the correct answer may ask the next question.

As each question is asked, place a checkmark by the corresponding term(s). Tell students that the same question may not be asked again, until each of the other terms have been used. This forces them to ask different kinds of questions and to look at each of the numbers in a variety of ways.

REPRODUCIBLE ACTIVITY PAGE (GRADES 2–5)

Answer Key: Answers will vary.

ASK AND ANSWER

Write five numbers in the boxes below. Then write six questions that can be answered by one or more of the numbers in the boxes. After each question, write the correct answer in parentheses.

Use the following terms:

     least

     greatest

     less than

     greater than

     greater than _____ and less than _____

     less than _____ and greater than _____

| 42 | 57 | 25 | 64 | 48 |

Which numbers are greater than 48? (57 and 64)

1. _____

_____

2. _____

_____

3. _____

_____

4. _____

_____

5. _____

_____

6. _____

_____

42   SPOKES OF SUMS

Materials needed:

chalkboard
chalk
eraser

☒ reproducible page
☒ total group activity
☐ individual activity
☒ partner activity

TOTAL GROUP ACTIVITY

Write a number between 8 and 20 on the chalkboard and draw a box around it. Draw spokes from each corner and from the middle of each side. Have students think of two numbers whose sum is the same as the number in the box. As each problem is said, write it near one of the spokes.

When eight solutions have been recorded, explain that there are other equally good answers, but you are going to write only eight answers (one for each spoke) so that the written work does not become too crowded.

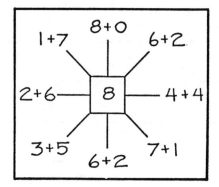

After working several puzzles together, you may wish to give students the "Spokes of Sums" Reproducible Activity Page to reinforce the concept.

PARTNER ADAPTATION (GRADES 2–3)

Materials needed:

"Spokes of Sums" reproducible activity page,
  several for each partner
pencils

Each partner takes a "Spokes of Sums" Reproducible Activity Page. One of the players names a number between 8 and 20. Both students write the number in the circle in the center of the first puzzle. They then race to see who can be the first to fill in all of the boxes with addition problems whose sums are the same as the number in the center.

Both players should complete *all* of the spokes for their puzzle. Next papers are exchanged and corrected. If all the problems in the puzzle are completed and correct, the student who finished first receives one point. If there are errors, the player does not receive a point. Instead, the other player receives the point, provided all his or her answers were correct. The loser of each turn names the next number.

The first person with a total of 3 points is the winner.

REPRODUCIBLE ACTIVITY PAGE (GRADES 2–3)

The reproducible activity page instructs students to write a number between 8 and 20 in the center circle of each puzzle and then to write addition problems the sums of which equal the number in the center. However, if students need added work on specific addition facts, you may wish to specify the numbers to be written in the circles.

This activity can be repeated many times by having students write different numbers in the center boxes each time they work on the page.

Answer Key: Answers will vary.

NAME

SPOKES OF SUMS

Write a number between 8 and 20 in each circle.
In each box, write an addition fact that equals the number in the circle.

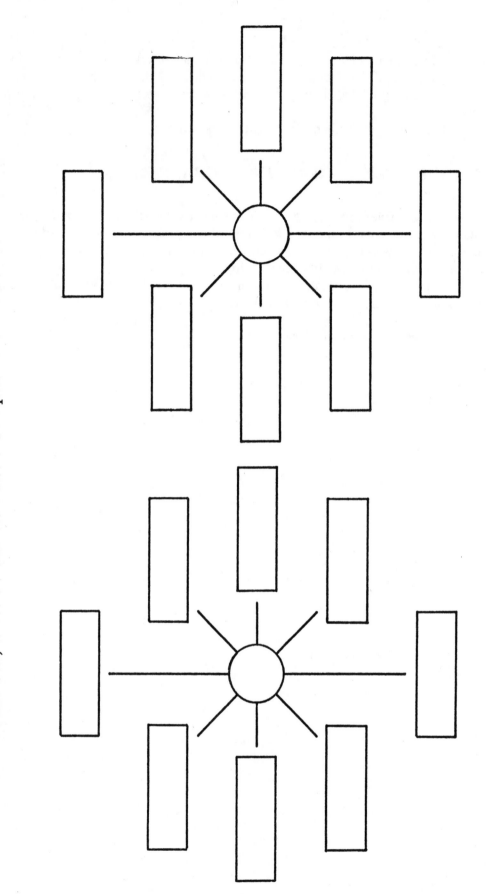

43   NUMBERS IN HIDING

Materials needed:

chalkboard
chalk
eraser

☒ reproducible page
☒ total group activity
☒ individual activity
☐ partner activity

TOTAL GROUP ACTIVITY

Write five numbers on the chalkboard. For example:

<u>12</u>   9   4   8   5

Ask students to solve the following problems:

1. The sum of which two numbers is 17? **(9, 8 or 12, 5)**
2. The difference between which two numbers is 8? **(12, 4)**
3. The sum of which two numbers is 16? **(12, 4)**
4. The difference between which two numbers is 7? **(12, 5)**
5. The sum of which three numbers is 18? **(9, 4, 5)**
6. Which numbers add up to 24? **(12, 8, 4)**
7. If you multiplied two numbers the answer would be 72. What are the two numbers? **(9, 8)**
8. If you multiplied two numbers and then added one number, the answer would be 37. What are the numbers? **(8 x 4) + 5**
9. If you multiplied two numbers and then subtracted one number, the answer would be 41. What are the numbers? **(9 x 5) − 4**

Erase the chalkboard. Write five new numbers and continue in the same manner using the problems from the sets on the pages that follow.

ADAPTATION FOR AN INDIVIDUAL STUDENT (GRADES 3–6)

Materials needed:

paper (6″ × 9″ for class book)
pencil

On a piece of 6″ × 9″ paper the student writes five numerals and a variety of questions like the ones above. The solution to each question is written on the back of the paper. When you have collected a sufficient number of these papers, they can be assembled into a class book of number puzzles for individual or whole-class use.

Find the Numbers

Set A: 13   7   4   6   11

1. The sum of which two numbers is 19? (13, 6)

2. The difference between which two numbers is 4? (11, 7)

3. The sum of which two numbers is 13? (7, 6)

4. The difference between which two numbers is 9? (13, 4)

5. The sum of which three numbers is 22? (7, 4, 11)

6. Which numbers add up to 30? (13, 7, 6, 4)

7. If you multiplied two numbers, the answer would be 42. What are the two numbers? (7, 6)

8. If you multiplied two numbers and then added one number, the answer would be 31. What are the numbers? $(6 \times 4) + 7$

9. If you multiplied two numbers and then subtracted one number, the answer would be 15. What are the numbers? $(7 \times 4) - 13$

Set B: 15   4   8   6   12

1. The sum of which two numbers is 21? (15, 6)

2. The difference between which two numbers is 8? (12, 4)

3. The sum of which two numbers is 20? (12, 8)

4. The difference between which two numbers is 3? (15, 12)

5. The sum of which three numbers is 24? (12, 4, 8)

6. Which numbers add up to 26? (8, 6, 12)

7. If you multiplied two numbers, the answer would be 32. What are the two numbers? (8, 4)

8. If you multiplied two numbers and then added one number, the answer would be 52. What are the numbers? $(8 \times 6) + 4$

9. If you multiplied two numbers and then subtracted one number, the answer would be 16. What are the numbers? $(6 \times 4) - 8$

Set C:	14	9	12	7	3

1. The sum of which two numbers is 15?   (12, 3)

2. The difference between which two numbers is 7?   (14, 7)

3. The sum of which two numbers is 26?   (14, 12)

4. The difference between which two numbers is 9?   (12, 3)

5. The sum of which three numbers is 28?   (12, 9, 7)

6. Which numbers add up to 31?   (9, 12, 7, 3)

7. If you multiplied two numbers, the answer would be 63. What are the two numbers?   (9, 7)

8. If you multiplied two numbers and then added one number, the answer would be 34. What are the numbers? $(9 \times 3) + 7$

9. If you multiplied two numbers and then subtracted one number, the answer would be 51. What are the numbers? $(9 \times 7) - 12$

Set D:	13	10	5	7	4

1. The sum of which two numbers is 20?   (13, 7)

2. The difference between which two numbers is 8?   (13, 5)

3. The sum of which two numbers is 12?   (7, 5)

4. The difference between which two numbers is 9?   (13, 4)

5. The sum of which three numbers is 25?   (13, 5, 7)

6. Which numbers add up to 26?   (10, 5, 7, 4)

7. If you multiplied two numbers, the answer would be 20. What are the two numbers?   (5, 4)

8. If you multiplied two numbers and then added one number, the answer would be 33. What are the numbers? $(7 \times 4) + 5$

9. If you multiplied two numbers and then subtracted one number, the answer would be 66. What are the numbers? $(10 \times 7) - 4$

REPRODUCIBLE ACTIVITY PAGE (GRADES 3–6)

Answer Key:

Set A

1. 16, 9
2. 16, 3
3. 14, 9
4. 3, 9, 7
5. 14, 3, 7
6. 9, 7
7. $(3 \times 9) + 14$
8. $(7 \times 3) - 14$

Set B

1. 16, 5
2. 12, 7
3. 16, 5
4. 16, 7, 5
5. 7, 5, 12
6. 7, 4
7. $(7 \times 4) + 16$
8. $(5 \times 4) - 16$

NAME _____

NUMBERS IN HIDING

Use the numbers in the boxes to answer the questions.

Set A:	14	3	9	16	7

1. The sum of which two numbers is 25? _____

2. The difference between which two numbers is 13? _____

3. The difference between which two numbers is 5? _____

4. The sum of which three numbers is 19? _____

5. Which numbers add up to 24? _____

6. If you multiplied two numbers, the answer
   would be 63. What are the two numbers? _____

7. If you multiplied two numbers, then added one number,
   the answer would be 41.
   What are the numbers? _____

8. If you multiplied two numbers and then subtracted one number,
   the answer would be 7.
   What are the numbers? _____

Set B:	16	7	5	12	4

1. The sum of which two numbers is 21? _____

2. The difference between which two numbers is 5? _____

3. The difference between which two numbers is 11? _____

4. The sum of which three numbers is 28? _____

5. Which numbers add up to 24? _____

6. If you multiplied two numbers, the answer
   would be 28. What are the two numbers? _____

7. If you multiplied two numbers, then added one number,
   the answer would be 44.
   What are the numbers? _____

8. If you multiplied two numbers and then subtracted one number,
   the answer would be 4.
   What are the numbers? _____

44   SUM SEARCH

Materials needed:

lined paper for each student
pencils
chalk
chalkboard
eraser

☒ reproducible page
☒ total group activity
☐ individual activity
☒ partner activity

TOTAL GROUP ACTIVITY

Draw a seven-column grid on the chalkboard and write six numerals between 1 and 20 at the top of the first six columns. Write "Total Sum" at the top of the seventh column. Tell students to copy the grid and numerals on lined paper.

Have students name a total of eight numbers between 20 and 100. As each of these is named, the students should write it in the right-hand column of their paper.

Challenge them to determine how many of the numbers in the right-hand column can be made by using the numerals at the top of each column. As each number is used, a check should be placed in the appropriate column, but no more than 5 checks may be placed in any one box.

1	3	6	11	15	18	total sum
✓		✓	✓	✓	✓	51
✓	✓	✓	✓		✓✓✓	93
✓			✓	✓		27

PARTNER ADAPTATION (GRADES 3–6)

Materials needed:

lined paper for each student
pencils

Each partner makes a seven column grid as described in the Total Group Activity. The players take turns naming six numbers between 1 and 20. Both students write these in the columns at the top of their grids, and label the seventh column "Total Sum."

Next they alternate naming five numbers between 20 and 100. These are written in the right-hand column.

For the next five minutes, each player searches for a way to make each of the numbers in the right-hand column. At the end of five minutes, the students check each other's papers. One point is awarded for each correct answer.

Students make a new grid and proceed in the same manner. The first player with 15 points, or the player who is ahead at the end of a designated time period, is the winner.

REPRODUCIBLE ACTIVITY PAGE (GRADES 3–6)

Answer Key: Answers will vary. One set of solutions follows:

2	9	5	7	11	13	TOTAL SUM
✓		✓	✓	✓✓		36
	✓		✓✓✓		✓	43
✓	✓✓			✓	✓✓	57
			✓✓	✓✓	✓✓	62
✓	✓	✓	✓	✓	✓	47
✓	✓✓✓		✓✓✓	✓		61
✓✓	✓	✓✓	✓		✓✓	56
✓✓✓		✓	✓✓✓	✓✓	✓	69
	✓✓	✓	✓✓	✓	✓✓	74
			✓✓✓	✓✓	✓✓✓	82
	✓	✓✓	✓	✓✓✓	✓✓	85
✓✓	✓✓	✓		✓✓✓	✓✓	99

Suggestion: If you do not have time to duplicate the reproducible activity page, as an alternate procedure have the students draw the grid as directed in the Total Group Activity, select their own numbers for the top row and right-hand column, and then work alone to see how many of the "number puzzles" they can solve.

SUM SEARCH

Total sums are listed in the right-hand column.
How many of the total sums can you make by
using the numbers at the top of the columns?

As each number is used, put a check in its column.
No more than 5 checks may be placed in any box.

1	6	11	15	18	total sum
✓	✓	✓	✓	✓	51
✓		✓	✓		21
✓	✓	✓✓✓		✓	58

2	9	5	7	11	13	TOTAL SUM
						36
						43
						57
						62
						47
						61
						56
						69
						74
						82
						85
						99

45   SO, WHAT'S THE NUMBER?

Materials needed:

½ sheet lined paper for each student
pencil for each student
optional: chalkboard, chalk, eraser

☒ reproducible page
☒ total group activity
☐ individual activity
☐ partner activity

TOTAL GROUP ACTIVITY

This activity provides practice in applying problem-solving skills.

Students should write their names at the top of a half sheet of lined paper. Explain that you will read a series of directions which they are to follow. As a visual reinforcement, you may want to write the numbers on the chalkboard as each direction and answer is given.

Instruct them as follows:

1. Write "93" on the top line.
2. Directly beneath the 93, write "– 37."
3. Subtract.
4. What is the answer? **(56)**
5. Skip a space.
6. Draw a line.
7. Below the line, write "77." This is the answer. Your job is to find out how I got this answer. — Did I multiply, divide, add, or subtract? —By how much? In the space write the number and the sign that will make the answer true. Then circle your answer. (+ 21)—**(Ask what number and sign they wrote to make certain they understand the directions. Have any student who has an incorrect answer correct it, so that all students are always working with the same numbers. Continue to follow this procedure as each answer is given.)**
8. Skip a space.
9. Draw a line.
10. Write "9." This is the answer. In the space, write how I got this answer. Then circle your answer. (– 68)—**(Ask what number and sign they wrote.)**

Steve

$$
\begin{array}{r}
8 \\
\cancel{93} \\
-37 \\
\hline
56 \\
\boxed{+21} \\
\hline
77 \\
\boxed{-68} \\
\hline
9 \\
\boxed{\times 8} \\
\hline
72 \\
\boxed{+35} \\
\hline
107 \\
\boxed{-100} \\
\hline
7 \\
\boxed{\times 7} \\
\hline
49 \\
\boxed{+49} \\
\hline
98 \\
\boxed{-35} \\
\hline
63 \\
\boxed{9} \overline{7}
\end{array}
$$

11. Skip a space.

12. Draw a line.

13. The answer is 72. Write it below the line. Fill in the blank and circle your answer. (x 8)— **(Ask what number and sign they wrote.)**

14. Skip a space.

15. Draw a line.

16. The answer is 107. Fill in the blank and circle your answer. (+ 35)—**(Ask what number and sign they wrote.)**

17. Skip a space.

18. Draw a line.

19. The answer is 7. Fill in the blank and circle your answer. (− 100)—**(Ask what number and sign they wrote.)**

20. Skip a space.

21. Draw a line.

22. The answer is 49. Fill in the blank and circle your answer. (x 7 or + 42)—**(Ask what number and sign they wrote.)**

23. Skip a space.

24. Draw a line.

25. The answer is 98. Fill in the blank and circle your answer. (x 2 or + 49)—**(Ask what number and sign they wrote.)**

26. Skip a space.

27. Draw a line.

28. The answer is 63. Fill in the blank and circle your answer. (− 35)—**(Ask what number and sign they wrote.)**

29. This is the last step. Make a division box under the "63." (If students are unfamiliar with the format used in the illustration to show the final division problem, briefly discuss this use of the "upside down division box.") Write a "7" under the "3" in "63." How did I get this final answer? Write your solution and circle it. (÷ 9)—**(Ask how they solved this last problem.)**

Here's another example to share with the students:

1. Write "47" on the top line.

2. Directly beneath the 47, write "+ 58."

3. Add.

4. What is the answer? **(105)**

5. Skip a space.

6. Draw a line.

7. Below the line, write "6." In the space, write how I got this answer and circle it. (− 99)— **(Ask for the answer.)**

8. Skip a space.

9. Draw a line.

10. Write "54." In the space, write your answer and circle it. (x 9 or + 48)—(Ask what number and sign they wrote.)

11. Skip a space.

12. Draw a line.

13. The answer is 108. Write it below the line. Fill in the blank and circle your answer. (+ 54 or x 2)— (Ask for the answer.)

14. Skip a space.

15. Draw a line.

16. The answer is 205. Fill in the blank and circle your answer. (+ 97)—(Ask what number and sign they wrote.)

17. Skip a space.

18. Draw a line.

19. The answer is 8. Fill in the blank and circle your answer. (− 197)—(Ask for the answer.)

20. Skip a space.

21. Draw a line.

22. The answer is 56. Fill in the blank and circle your answer. (x 7 or + 48)—(Ask what number and sign they wrote.)

23. Skip a space.

24. Draw a line.

25. The answer is 150. Fill in the blank and circle your answer. (+ 94)—(Ask for the answer.)

26. Skip a space.

27. Draw a line.

28. The answer is 42. Fill in the blank and circle your answer. (− 108)—(Ask what number and sign they wrote.)

29. This is the last step. Make a division box under the "42." Write a "7" under the "2" in "42." How did I get this final answer? Write your solution and circle it. (÷ 6)—(Ask how they solved the last problem.)

Stephanie

$$47$$
$$+ 58$$
$$105$$
$$- 99$$
$$6$$
$$\times 9$$
$$54$$
$$+ 54$$
$$108$$
$$+ 97$$
$$205$$
$$- 197$$
$$8$$
$$\times 7$$
$$56$$
$$+ 94$$
$$150$$
$$- 108$$
$$6\overline{)42}$$
$$7$$

REPRODUCIBLE ACTIVITY PAGE (GRADES 4–6)

Answer Key:

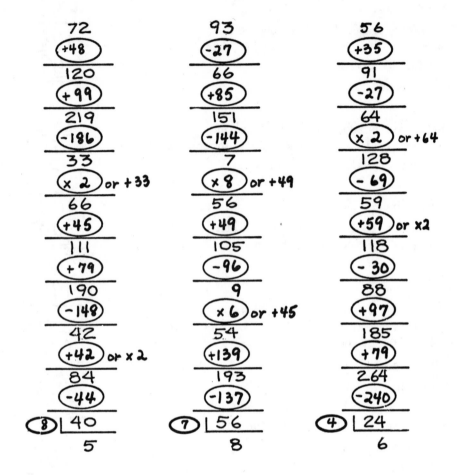

NAME _____

SO, WHAT'S THE NUMBER?

Fill in each oval so that the answer just below it is true.

Column 1

72
(48)
120
( )
219
( )
33
( )
66
( )
111
( )
190
( )
42
( )
84
( )
( ) ⌐40
5

Column 2

93
( )
66
( )
151
( )
7
( )
56
( )
105
( )
9
( )
54
( )
193
( )
( ) ⌐56
8

Column 3

56
( )
91
( )
64
( )
128
( )
59
( )
118
( )
88
( )
185
( )
264
( )
( ) ⌐24
6

46   TARGET NUMBER

Materials needed:

unlined paper for each student
pencils
chalkboard
chalk
eraser

☒ reproducible page
☒ total group activity
☐ individual activity
☐ partner activity

TOTAL GROUP ACTIVITY

This activity provides practice in applying problem-solving skills.
On the chalkboard write the following:

TARGET NUMBER: 5

| 4 | 3 | 7 | 5 |

Tell students they are to try to reach the target number by using the numbers you have written on the chalkboard. They may multiply, divide, add, or subtract. All of the numbers must be used. However, each number may be used once and only once.

Explain that it may take many tries before they find a solution. For example, they might try $(7 + 5) \div 4 + 3$. This is close, but not close enough! As a result they would need to try other ways of combining the numbers.

Students may write out their various trials or work through them mentally. However, their final solution should be written, so that it is not forgotten. Ask students to circle their last number, the Target Number. If some students finish before the others, encourage them to seek additional solutions to the puzzle.

One possible solution is listed for each puzzle, but students should share all of the solutions they discover.

After working the first introductory four-number puzzle, you may want to write one of the five-number puzzles on the following page on the chalkboard, and let students work throughout the day on solving it. Or it could be assigned as challenge homework.

Can You Solve These Puzzles?

A. TARGET NUMBER: 7 6　8　5　2　4	**B.** TARGET NUMBER: 12 3　7　5　9　6
C. TARGET NUMBER: 24 6　9　8　4　5	**D.** TARGET NUMBER: 5 6　9　5　8　7
E. TARGET NUMBER: 4 8　6　7　3　9	**F.** TARGET NUMBER: 21 9　6　8　4　3

Solutions: (Accept all solutions that follow the rules.)

```
A.   5      B.   5      C.   6      D.   6      E.   7      F.   4
    +4          ×3          ×4          ×5          +9          ×6
   ----        ----        ----        ----        ----        ----
     9          15          24          30          16          24
    ×6          +6          -9          +7          -8          -9
   ----        ----        ----        ----        ----        ----
    54         7⌊21        5⌊15         37           8          15
    +2           3           3          +8          ×3          -8
   ----         +9          ×8         ----        ----        ----
   8⌊56        ----        ----        9⌊45        6⌊24          7
    (7)         +9          ×8          (5)         (4)         ×3
               (12)        (24)                                ----
                                                               (21)
```

REPRODUCIBLE ACTIVITY PAGE (GRADES 4–6)

Provide unlined paper for students to use when trying various solutions to the puzzles.

Answer Key: One possible solution for each problem follows, but all solutions should be accepted that reach the target number by using each number once and only once.

```
    A.   4      B.   3      C.   3
        +8          ×7          ×6
       ----        ----        ----
       2⌊12         21          18
         6          +9          -9
        ×3         ----        ----
       9⌊18        5⌊30          9
        (2)          6          -5
                    +2         ----
                   ----        2⌊4
                    (8)         (2)
```

TARGET NUMBER

For each puzzle, use the numbers in the boxes to try to reach the TARGET NUMBER. You may add, subtract, multiply, or divide. Each number should be used one time, but numbers may not be used more than one time. In the space below, show how you reached the target number.

A.   TARGET NUMBER: 2

9   2   8   3   4

B.   TARGET NUMBER: 8

2   7   5   9   3

C.   TARGET NUMBER: 2

6   2   3   5   9

47   BREAK MY CODE

Materials needed:

chalkboard
chalk
eraser

☒ reproducible page
☒ total group activity
☒ individual activity
☐ partner activity

TOTAL GROUP ACTIVITY

Tell students you are going to write a number puzzle on the chalkboard, but it's going to be written in code. They are to try to break your code and solve the puzzle.

On the chalkboard write:

$$\boxed{\begin{matrix} X\ X \\ X \end{matrix}} = 15 \qquad \boxed{\begin{matrix} \bullet\ \bullet \\ X \end{matrix}} = 11$$

Ask students who think they can determine the value of "**X**" and "•" (**X** = 5; • = 3), to raise their hands, but tell them *not* to give away the code. Then write:

Therefore:

A. $\boxed{\begin{matrix} \bullet\ \bullet\ \bullet \\ X\ X \end{matrix}} = ?$ Ask for a volunteer to write or give the answer to problem A. (19)

Follow with other problems, asking students to give the answer after each one. Then have them discuss how they broke the code. (Answers: B = 18, C = 17, D = 23, E = 16)

(If three "X"s equaled 15, "X" had to have the value of 5. By substituting 5 for the "X" in the next puzzle and knowing that 5 + 6 equals 11, each "•" had to be worth 3.)

B. $\boxed{\begin{matrix} X\ X \\ X\ \bullet \end{matrix}} = ?$ C. $\boxed{\begin{matrix} X\ \bullet\ \bullet \\ \bullet\ \bullet \end{matrix}} = ?$

D. $\boxed{\begin{matrix} X\ \bullet\ X \\ X\ X \end{matrix}} = ?$ E. $\boxed{\begin{matrix} X\ X \\ \bullet\ \bullet \end{matrix}} = ?$

Continue in the same way, using the puzzles that follow.

$$\boxed{\begin{matrix} \bullet\ \bullet \\ \bullet\ \bullet \end{matrix}} = 16 \\ \boxed{\begin{matrix} \bullet\ X \\ X\ X \end{matrix}} = 13$$

Therefore!

A. $\boxed{\begin{matrix} X\ \bullet \\ \bullet \end{matrix}} = ?$ C. $\boxed{\begin{matrix} X \\ \bullet\ \bullet\ \bullet \end{matrix}} = ?$

B. $\boxed{\begin{matrix} \bullet\ \bullet \\ X\ X \end{matrix}} = ?$ D. $\boxed{\begin{matrix} \bullet\ \bullet \\ X\ X \end{matrix}} = ?$

Answers: • = 4, X = 3; A = 11, B = 14, C = 15, D = 17

139

Therefore:

A. ●● / X X = ?   C. X X / ●●● = ?

●● = 4 }

X ● / ●● = 12 }

B. ●● / X = ?   D. X X / X ● = ?

Answers: ● = 2, X = 6; A = 16, B = 10, C = 18, D = 20

Therefore

X X X / X X = 20 }

A. ●● / X = ?   C. X X / X ● = ?

X X / ●● = 28 }

B. X ● / ●● = ?   D. X ● / ●● = ?

Answers: ● = 10, X = 4; A = 24, B = 34, C = 22, D = 44

(Teachers will find puzzles of this type, plus many other math activities in *The Mathworks*, © 1978, Creative Publications, Palo Alto, CA 94903.)

ADAPTATION FOR AN INDIVIDUAL STUDENT (GRADES 4–6)

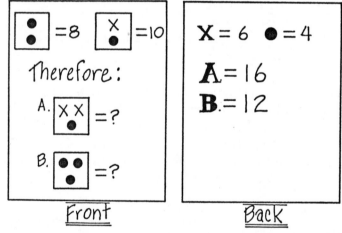

Materials needed:

unlined 6″ x 9″ paper
pencil

Have the student write a puzzle and two problems on one side on a piece of unlined 6″ x 9″ paper. The solution to the puzzle and the answers to the problems should be written on the reverse side. When you have collected a sufficient number of these papers, assemble them into a class book of code puzzles.

REPRODUCIBLE ACTIVITY PAGE (GRADES 4–6)

Answer Key: 1. X = 5, □ = 4   2. X = 3, □ = 9   3. X = 7, □ = 4
              A = 16   E = 33   I = 29
              B = 22   F = 21   J = 15
              C = 23   G = 21   K = 19
              D = 19   H = 27   L = 26

NAME _____

BREAK MY CODE

Use the Coded Answers to discover what the "X" equals and what the "□" equals. Then use these numbers to find the value of each puzzle.

CODED ANSWERS

X X / X = 15

□ □ / X = 13

X = _____   □ = _____
Therefore!

A. = _____   C. = _____

B. = _____   D. = _____

CODED ANSWERS

□ □ / □ □ = 36

X □ / □ □ = 30

X = _____   □ = _____
Therefore!

E. = _____   F. = _____

G. = _____   H. = _____

CODED ANSWERS

X X / X X = 28

□ □ / X = 23

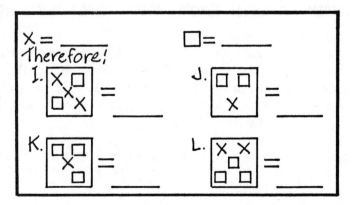

X = _____   □ = _____
Therefore!

I. = _____   J. = _____

K. = _____   L. = _____

	48 HOW MANY WORDS PER PAGE?

Materials needed:

chalkboard
chalk
eraser
lined paper for each student
pencils
one book that contains full pages of
    text for each student (science or social studies
    books work well)

☒ reproducible page
☒ total group activity
☐ individual activity
☐ partner activity

TOTAL GROUP ACTIVITY

Open a textbook to any page and ask students how they might estimate the number of words on the page. Suggestions might include:

1. **Count the words** in one line and multiply that number by the number of lines on the page.

2. **Find the number** of words in "five" lines. Divide by "five" to determine the average number of words in these lines. Then multiply this by the number of lines on the page.

3. **Count the number** of words in one sentence. Multiply it by the number of sentences on the page.

Have them estimate the number of words on the page by using each method, recording their answers on the chalkboard after each calculation.

While they are working on the problem, count the actual number of words on the page. When all methods have been tried, reveal the true number, so they can determine which method produced the most accurate result.

If time permits, have them turn to a different page and repeat the calculations, challenging them to discover whether any one method consistently proves effective.

REPRODUCIBLE ACTIVITY PAGE (GRADES 5–6)

If you use this page with the total class, have students randomly select a full page of text from a book. Students should not all use the same book, so that the results of the three "formulas" for estimating the number of words per page can be applied to a variety of material.

When they have completed the page, discuss results and have them determine whether any method proved to be more accurate.

Answer Key: Answers will vary, but students' calculations should be checked for accuracy.

HOW MANY WORDS PER PAGE?

Turn to a *full page of text* in a book. Use all three methods listed below to estimate the number of words on the page.

METHOD 1

1. Count the number of words in *one line.* _____

2. Count the number of lines on the page. _____

3. Multiply these two numbers to estimate the total number of words on the page.

4. Write the estimate. _____

METHOD 2

1. Count the number of words in *five lines.* _____

2. Divide this number by 5 to find the *average* number of words in *each of the five lines.*

3. Multiply your answer by the number of lines on the page. This will give you another estimate of the number of words on the entire page.

4. Write the estimate. _____

METHOD 3

1. Count the number of words in *one sentence.* _____

2. Count the number of *sentences* on the page. _____

3. Multiply these two numbers to get a third estimate of the number of words on the page.

4. Write the estimate. _____

1. Now count how many words are really on the page. _____

2. Circle the method that gave the most accurate estimate.

| METHOD 1 | METHOD 2 | METHOD 3 |

49   CODE CHALLENGE

Materials needed:

chalkboard
chalk
eraser
lined paper for each student
pencils

☒ reproducible page
☒ total group activity
☐ individual activity
☐ partner activity

TOTAL GROUP ACTIVITY

This activity gives students practice in doing mental math.

Draw the following diagram of a "code box" on the chalkboard, and have students copy it on paper.

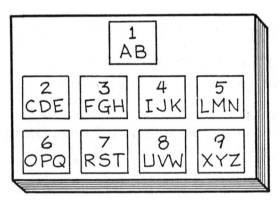

Have students determine the value of a word by looking at the "code box" to find out how much each letter is worth. They should *mentally* add the numbers to find the total value, then write their answer on paper.

Mental calculation:

$$
\begin{aligned}
s &= 7 \\
u &= 8 \\
s &= 7 \\
p &= 6 \\
e &= 2 \\
n &= 5 \\
s &= 7 \\
e &= 2 \\
\hline
\end{aligned}
$$

44 TOTAL CODE VALUE

Ask if anyone can find a word with the value of 24.

Example:

$$
\begin{aligned}
q &= 6 \\
u &= 8 \\
i &= 4 \\
c &= 2 \\
k &= 4 \\
\hline
\end{aligned}
$$

24 TOTAL

Who can find a word with the value of 17?

Who can find the word with the largest value?

What is the value of their first and last name?

Which has a higher total code value, *science* or *English*?

What is the value of each word when its sum is multipled by the value of the last letter in the word?

ADAPTATION FOR AN INDIVIDUAL STUDENT (GRADES 3–6)

Materials needed:

lined paper

pencil

Have the student copy the above chart at the top of a page and use it to write coded messages. When you have collected a sufficient number of these papers, assemble them into a book that can be enjoyed by the class.

REPRODUCIBLE ACTIVITY PAGE (GRADES 3–6)

Answer Key: A: (1) 29, (2) 25, (3) 37, (4) 45, (5) 27, (6) 35, (7) 40, (8) 21, (9) 53, (10) 60; B: (1) 34, (2) 34, (3) 26, (4) 30, (5) 41, (6) 26, (7) 23, (8) 27, (9) 47, (10) 36. Highest value in each column: A, strawberries; B, volleyball.

Suggestion: If you do not have time to duplicate the reproducible page, write ten words on the chalkboard and have students find the value of each, or challenge students to find the highest valued five-letter word, six-lettered word, etc.

NAME _____

CODE CHALLENGE

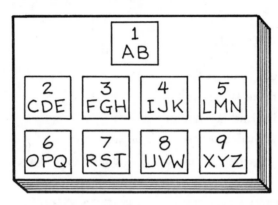

What is the value of the words below? Look at the code box to find out how much the letters in each word are worth. *Mentally* add the numbers to find the total value. Then write your answer.

I'm worth 28 points!!

Challenge

Circle the food in Set A that you *think* will have the highest value.

Set A	Total Value
1. pizza	
2. ice cream	
3. hamburger	
4. french fries	
5. hot dog	
6. milkshake	
7. fried chicken	
8. steak	
9. watermellon	
10. strawberries	

Circle the sport in Set B that you *think* will have the highest value.

Set B	Total Value
1. basketball	
2. football	
3. soccer	
4. tennis	
5. swimming	
6. hockey	
7. baseball	
8. skiing	
9. volleyball	
10. badminton	

Which food in Set A had the highest value? _____

Which sport in Set B had the highest value? _____

©1989 by The Center for Applied Research in Education

50   FIND MY VALUE

Materials needed:

chalkboard
chalk
eraser
lined paper for each student
pencils

☒ reproducible page
☒ total group activity
☒ individual activity
☐ partner activity

TOTAL GROUP ACTIVITY

On the chalkboard write the letters "A" through "M." Number from 1 to 13, placing a numeral under each letter. Have students copy this while you write "N" through "Z" and once more number from 1 to 13.

A	B	C	D	E	F	G	H	I	J	K	L	M
1	2	3	4	5	6	7	8	9	10	11	12	13

N	O	P	Q	R	S	T	U	V	W	X	Y	Z
1	2	3	4	5	6	7	8	9	10	11	12	13

Write a word on the chalkboard, and ask students to determine its "value" by looking at their chart to see what each letter is worth and then adding the total.

Example: "math"   m = 13
                      a = 1
                      t = 7
                      h = 8
                      _____
                      29 TOTAL

Have them find the value of various words, including their first names.

Variation

To provide multiplication *and* additional practice, have students find the value of a word and then multiply it by the value of the last letter.

REPRODUCIBLE ACTIVITY PAGE (GRADES 3–6)

Provide scrap paper for students to use while making their calculations.

Answer Key: Answers will vary.

FIND MY VALUE

In this activity you must think of words that are worth a certain number of points. Use the chart to find out how much each letter is worth. Then think of a word that has the total value listed below. The word should be written in the boxes, one letter per box, but it does *not* need to fill all of the boxes. Write the value of the letters in the boxes below the word.

A	B	C	D	E	F	G	H	I	J	K	L	M
1	2	3	4	5	6	7	8	9	10	11	12	13

N	O	P	Q	R	S	T	U	V	W	X	Y	Z
1	2	3	4	5	6	7	8	9	10	11	12	13

1. Write a word with a value of 60.

word											
value of each letter											

2. Write your first name. What is its total value? _____

name											
value of each letter											

3. Write your last name. What is its total value? _____

name											
value of each letter											

4. Which of your names has a higher value? _____

5. Which school subject has the highest value when you use this chart? Write the name of the subject and its total value.

school subject											TOTAL VALUE
value of each letter											

51 PALINDROMES

Materials needed:

chalkboard
chalk
eraser
½ sheet of lined paper
for each student
pencils

☒ reproducible page
☒ total group activity
☐ individual activity
☐ partner activity

TOTAL GROUP ACTIVITY

Palindromes are words, phrases, or numbers that are the same when read either forward or backward. Examples of palindromic numbers include 13431 and 783387. Students enjoy searching for these numbers, and in the process, they receive a great deal of practice adding large numbers.

Explain palindromes, then write the number 877 on the chalkboard. Tell students they are going to help you turn this into a palindromic number. Have them read the number to you in reverse order. Write the new number directly under the first one.

$$\begin{array}{r} 877 \\ +778 \\ \hline 1655 \end{array}$$ Add a plus sign, and add the two numbers.

Ask if this is a palindromic number. Have students reverse the new number. Write it under the previous number, and add them. Continue until the result is a palindrome. (The number 877 requires four steps.)

$$\begin{array}{r} 877 \\ +778 \\ \hline 1655 \\ +5561 \\ \hline 7216 \\ +6127 \\ \hline 13343 \\ +34331 \\ \hline 47674 \end{array}$$

Step 1

Step 2

Step 3

Step 4

When students understand the concept, give them lined paper. Write a number on the chalkboard and have them turn it into a palindrome. They should circle the final sum and write the number of steps that were necessary. Explain that they can quickly determine the number of steps by counting the number of plus signs or the number of horizontal lines.

Find the...Palindromic Numbers

3-STEP NUMBERS	FINAL NUMBER	4-STEP NUMBERS	FINAL NUMBER
554	11011	995	22022
786	9339	579	23232
348	5115	769	67276
194	2992	290	2552
461	2662	699	46464
934	9119	947	68486
751	8888	192	6996
277	15851	789	88088
983	7117	280	2662
284	4774	927	69696
397	7557	819	89298
663	13431	480	13431
165	484	789	66066
86	1111		
483	6996	**5-STEP NUMBERS**	**FINAL NUMBER**
180	747	176	44044
382	2552	945	59895
650	4444	738	99099
845	9559	562	45254
349	7337	297	79497
750	6666		
892	3113	**6-STEP NUMBERS**	**FINAL NUMBER**
		988	881188
4-STEP NUMBERS	**FINAL NUMBER**	799	449944
174	5115	97	44044
728	45254	182	45254
976	47674	977	475574
78	4884		
571	9559	**7-STEP NUMBERS**	**FINAL NUMBER**
847	44044	782	233332
294	9339	296	881188
638	25652	190	45254

REPRODUCIBLE ACTIVITY PAGE (GRADES 4–6)

Answer Key:
786, 3 steps, 9339
182, 6 steps, 45254
699, 4 steps, 46464
688, 8 steps, 1136311
945, 5 steps, 59895
296, 7 steps, 881188

Suggestion: If you do not have time to duplicate the reproducible page, as an alternate procedure assign seven to ten numbers from the list on the previous page. Students should turn each into a palindromic number, recording the number of steps that were necessary and the final number.

NAME _____

PALINDROMES

Palindromes are words, phrases, or numbers that are the same when read either forward or backward. Examples of palindromic numbers include 13431 and 783387.

Any number can be turned into a palindromic number. Here's how to do it.

Step 1. $\left\{\begin{array}{r} 877 \\ +778 \end{array}\right.$

Step 2. $\left\{\begin{array}{r} 1655 \\ +5561 \end{array}\right.$

Step 3. $\left\{\begin{array}{r} 7216 \\ +6127 \end{array}\right.$

Step 4. $\left\{\begin{array}{r} 13343 \\ +34331 \end{array}\right.$

Palindromic Number: $\overline{47674}$

- Write a number.
- Write the same number *in reverse order* just beneath the first number.
- Add a plus sign and write the total of the two numbers.
- If the sum is not a palindrome, reverse this number. Write it under the previous number, and add them together.
- Continue reversing numbers and adding, until the result is a palindrome.

Turn each of the following numbers into a palindrome. Work the problems on a separate piece of paper. Then fill in the chart below, showing how many steps were needed, and the resulting palindromic number.

(You can easily find out the number of steps that were taken by counting the number of plus signs.)

None of the numbers below require more then eight steps.

Start With	Number of Steps	Final Palindromic Number
877	4	47674
786		
182		
699		
688		
945		
296		

52   MAGIC 4

Materials needed:
½ sheet of lined paper for each student
pencils

[X] reproducible page
[X] total group activity
[ ] individual activity
[ ] partner activity

TOTAL GROUP ACTIVITY

This activity provides practice in addition, subtraction, and division by 2.
Each student chooses a different starting number, but everyone ends with the very same answer!

Read the following directions to the students.

1. Choose any number and write it on your paper.
2. Double your number.
3. Add 15.
4. Subtract 7.
5. Divide by 2.
6. Subtract your original number.
   (At this point, all students should have 4 as an answer, but for now pretend that you don't know.)

```
   263
 +263
  526
 + 15
  541
 -  7
2)534
  267
 -263
    4
```

Remind them that they all started with different numbers. Ask one student to read his or her answer and casually ask if anyone else has the same answer. Then watch the amazement on the other students' faces as they realize they all have identical answers. This is a good time to distribute the accompanying reproducible activity page, so they can practice the trick. Later they can have fun trying it on others.

REPRODUCIBLE ACTIVITY PAGE (GRADES 3–6)

Answer Key: The final answer should be 4.

MAGIC 4

Work each step of the magic trick, writing your answers in the space on the left-hand side of the paper.

Then do the trick again, starting with a *different number*. This time write in the space on the right-hand side of the paper.

When you are sure the magic trick works, try it on someone else. Have the person secretly write a number—any number. Then announce that you will name the person's secret number at the end of the trick.

FIRST TRY	DIRECTIONS	SECOND TRY
←	1. Write any number. (First try) (Second try)	→
	2. Double your number.	
	3. Add 15.	
	4. Subtract 7.	
	5. Divide by 2.	
	6. Subtract your original number.	
	The remaining number should be 4.	

53 PICK ANOTHER NUMBER

Materials needed:

½ sheet of lined paper for each student
pencils

[X] reproducible page
[X] total group activity
[ ] individual activity
[ ] partner activity

TOTAL GROUP ACTIVITY

This activity provides practice in addition, subtraction, and multiplication by 5 and 10.

Read the following directions to the students.

1. Select a secret number between 1 and 99, and write it on your paper.
2. Multiply your number by 10.
3. Add 57.
4. Double your new number.
5. Subtract 91.
6. Multiply by 5.
7. Add 100.
8. Tell me your answer, and I will tell you your secret number.

$$
\begin{array}{r}
92 \\
\times\,10 \\
\hline
920 \\
+\ 57 \\
\hline
977 \\
+977 \\
\hline
1954 \\
-\ 91 \\
\hline
1863 \\
\times\ \ 5 \\
\hline
9315 \\
+100 \\
\hline
9415
\end{array}
$$

To determine the secret number, mentally drop the last two digits off the student's answer. Then subtract 2. (Or, you may find it easier to listen *only* to the first two digits of the answer, and subtract 2 from this.)

$$
\begin{array}{r}
94\cancel{1}\cancel{5} \\
-\ 2 \\
\hline
92
\end{array}
$$

After telling several students their secret number, you may want to give them the accompanying reproducible activity page, so they can do the magic trick with others.

REPRODUCIBLE ACTIVITY PAGE (GRADES 3–6)

Answer Key: Answers will vary, but the final number should be the same as the starting number.

PICK ANOTHER NUMBER

pick a number!

Work each step of the magic trick, writing your answers in the space on the left-hand side of the paper.

Then do the trick again, starting with a different number. This time write in the space on the right-hand side of the paper.

When you are sure the magic trick works, try it on someone else. Have the person secretly write a number between 1 and 99. Then announce that you will name the person's secret number at the end of the trick.

FIRST TRY	DIRECTIONS	SECOND TRY
←	1. Write a number between 1 and 99. (First try) (Second try)	→
	2. Multiply your number by 10.	
	3. Add 57.	
	4. Double your new number.	
	5. Subtract 91.	
	6. Multiply by 5.	
	7. Add 100.	
	8. When you are trying this trick on someone else say, "Tell me your answer, and I will tell you your secret number."	
	9. To find the secret number, cross off the last two digits of the answer. Then subtract 2.	

54   ABRACADABRA

Materials needed:

½ sheet of lined paper for each student
pencils

☒ reproducible page
☒ total group activity
☐ individual activity
☐ partner activity

TOTAL GROUP ACTIVITY

This activity provides practice in addition, subtraction, and division by 2.

Students select a number with any number of digits. Before they follow a series of directions, tell them that you already know that the answer is 3, if they calculate correctly.

Read the following directions to the students.

1. Select any number and write it on your paper.
2. Add 9 to your number.
3. Double your new number.
4. Subtract 12.
5. Divide by 2.
6. Subtract the number you originally selected.
   (**With no errors, 3 is the answer.**)

$$
\begin{array}{r}
37 \\
+\ 9 \\
\hline
46 \\
+46 \\
\hline
92 \\
-12 \\
\hline
2\,|\,80 \\
40 \\
-37 \\
\hline
3
\end{array}
$$

REPRODUCIBLE ACTIVITY PAGE (GRADES 3–6)

Answer Key: The final answer should be 3.

ABRACADABRA

Work each step of the magic trick, writing your answers in the space on the left-hand side of the paper.

Then do the trick again, starting with a different number. This time write in the space on the right-hand side of the paper.

When you are sure the magic trick works, try it on someone else. Have the person secretly write a number—any number. Then announce that before you even start you will name the person's final answer. It will be 3.

Abracadabra!

FIRST TRY	DIRECTIONS	SECOND TRY
←	1. Select any number and write it on your paper. (First try) (Second try)	→
	2. Add 9 to your number.	
	3. Double your new number.	
	4. Subtract 12.	
	5. Divide by 2.	
	6. Subtract the number you originally selected.	
	The remaining number should be 3.	

55 MORE HOCUS POCUS

Materials needed:

½ sheet of lined paper for each student and
  for the teacher
pencils

[X] reproducible page
[X] total group activity
[ ] individual activity
[ ] partner activity

TOTAL GROUP ACTIVITY

This activity provides practice in addition and multiplication.

Tell students that you are going to use this "magic trick" to find out how many people are in their families and how many brothers and sisters they have. Before starting you may want to decide on a definition for "family." They could count the number of people living in their household, or they could count brothers and sisters (at home or away from home) plus their parent(s).

Read the following directions to the students.

1. Write the number of people in your family.
2. Multiply this number by 4.
3. Add 10.
4. Multiply by 25.
5. How many brothers and sisters do you have? Add that number.
6. Add the number of days in a year. (365)
7. Tell me your answer, and I'll tell you how many people are in your family and how many brothers and sisters you have.

```
    5 (number of people
  X 4      in family)
  ─────
   20
 + 10
  ─────
   30
 X 25
  ─────
  150
   60
  ─────
  750
 +  3 (number of brothers
  ─────    and sisters)
  753
 +365
  ─────
 1118
```

When a student tells you his or her answer, write it on your paper, then subtract 615. Draw a line on either side of the zero in the tens place.

```
   1118
 -  615
  ─────
   5|0|3
```
number of people   number of brothers
  in family   and sisters

The number(s) on the left tell you how many people are in the student's family. The number(s) on the right indicate the number of brothers and sisters.

After telling several students about the composition of their families, you may want to tell the others the secret and then distribute the accompanying reproducible page, so they can do the magic trick with others.

REPRODUCIBLE ACTIVITY PAGE (GRADES 4–6)

Answer Key: Answers will vary.

MORE HOCUS POCUS

Practice each step of the magic trick, writing your answers in the space on the right-hand side of the paper.

When you are sure the magic trick works, try it on someone else. Before you start, announce that at the end of the trick you will tell how many brothers and sisters the person has and how many people are in his or her family. Then have the person follow your directions, being careful to secretly write each number so that you can't see it.

Let's see. There are five people in your family, and you have three brothers and sisters.

$$\begin{array}{r} 1118 \\ -615 \\ \hline 5|0|3 \end{array}$$

DIRECTIONS	
1. Write the number of people in your family.	
2. Multiply this number by 4.	
3. Add 10.	
4. Multiply by 25.	
5. How many brothers and sisters do you have? Add that number.	
6. Add the number of days in a year. (365)	
7. When you are trying this trick on someone else say, "Tell me your answer, and I'll tell you how many people are in your family and how many brothers and sisters you have."	
8. When the person tells you his or her answer, write it on a piece of paper. Then subtract 615.	
9. Draw a line on either side of the zero in the tens place.	
10. The number(s) on the left tell you how many people are in the person's family. The number(s) on the right tell you how many brothers and sisters the person has. (See the illustration at the top of the page.)	

56   WE'RE STUCK ON 11

Materials needed:

½ sheet of lined paper for each student
pencils

- [X] reproducible page
- [X] total group activity
- [ ] individual activity
- [ ] partner activity

TOTAL GROUP ACTIVITY

This activity provides practice in addition, subtraction, multiplication, and division.

Have students work the following series of calculations several times, each time starting with a different number. They are amazed to discover that regardless of what number they use at the beginning, their final answer is always 11.

Read the following directions to the students.

1. Choose a secret number that is larger than 3 (any number of digits) and write it on your paper.
2. Add 13.
3. Multiply your new number by 6.
4. Subtract 15.
5. Divide by 3.
6. Subtract 4 less than your secret number.
7. Subtract 3 more than your secret number.
8. Divide by 2.

$$
\begin{array}{r}
457 \\
+\ \ 13 \\
\hline
470 \\
\times\ \ \ 6 \\
\hline
2820 \\
-\ \ 15 \\
\hline
3\,|\,2805 \\
935 \\
-453 \\
\hline
482 \\
-460 \\
\hline
2\,|\,22 \\
11
\end{array}
$$

They should all have 11 as an answer, but tell them not to give their answer away. Instead have them select a new number and repeat the above steps. When they are finished say, "Don't say anything to anyone, but check and see if you had the same answer as before. Let's try it one more time. Start with a new number and see what happens."

REPRODUCIBLE ACTIVITY PAGE (GRADES 4–6)

Answer Key: The final answer should be 11.

WE'RE STUCK ON 11

Work each step of the magic trick, writing your answers in the space on the left-hand side of the paper.

Then do the trick again, starting with a different number. This time write in the space on the right-hand side of the paper.

When you are sure the magic trick works, try it on someone else. Have the person secretly write a number that is larger than 3—any number that is larger than 3. Then announce that you will name the person's secret number at the end of the trick.

FIRST TRY	DIRECTIONS	SECOND TRY
←	1. Choose a secret number that is larger than 3 and write it on your paper. (First try)　(Second try) →	
	2. Add 13.	
	3. Multiply your new number by 6.	
	4. Subtract 15.	
	5. Divide by 3.	
	6. Subtract 4 less than your secret number.	
	7. Subtract 3 more than your secret number.	
	8. Divide by 2.	
	—————————— The remaining number should be 11.	

©1989 by The Center for Applied Research in Education

57 THE 280 TRICK

Materials needed:

½ sheet of lined paper for each student
pencils

☒ reproducible page
☒ total group activity
☐ individual activity
☐ partner activity

TOTAL GROUP ACTIVITY

This activity provides practice in addition, subtraction, and multiplication.

Have each student choose a number—any number. Direct everyone to make the following series of calculations. Then watch their surprise when they discover that although they began with different numbers, everyone's final number is the same as the one they initially selected.

Read the following directions to the students.

1. Select a secret number and write it on your paper.
2. Multiply your number by 2.
3. Add 3.
4. Multiply your new number by 5.
5. Add 13.
6. Multiply this number by 10.
7. Subtract 280.
8. Cross off the final two zeros.
9. Compare the number you have now with your secret number. (The numbers should be the same.)

$$\begin{array}{r} 389 \\ \times\ \ 2 \\ \hline 778 \\ +\ \ 3 \\ \hline 781 \\ \times\ \ 5 \\ \hline 3905 \\ +\ \ 13 \\ \hline 3918 \\ \times\ \ 10 \\ \hline 39180 \\ -\ 280 \\ \hline 38900 \end{array}$$

REPRODUCIBLE ACTIVITY PAGE (GRADES 4–6)

Answer Key: Answers will vary, but the final number should be the same as the beginning number.

THE 280 TRICK

Work each step of the magic trick, writing your answers in the space on the left-hand side of the paper.

Then do the trick again, starting with a different number. This time write in the space on the right-hand side of the paper.

When you are sure the magic trick works, try it on someone else. Have the person secretly write a number—any number. Then announce that you will have the person multiply, add, and subtract from this number. But before you even begin, you will name the final answer. It will be the same number as the one the person just wrote.

FIRST TRY	DIRECTIONS	SECOND TRY
←	1. Select a secret number and write it on your paper. (First try) (Second try)	→
	2. Multiply your number by 2.	
	3. Add 3.	
	4. Multiply your new number by 5.	
	5. Add 13.	
	6. Multiply this number by 10.	
	7. Subtract 280.	
	8. Cross off the final two zeros.	
	9. Compare the number you have now with your secret number. They should be exactly the same.	

©1989 by The Center for Applied Research in Education

58 INSTANT SUMS

Materials needed:

chalkboard
chalk
eraser
½ sheet of lined paper for each student
pencils

- [X] reproducible page
- [X] total group activity
- [ ] individual activity
- [ ] partner activity

TOTAL GROUP ACTIVITY

This "magic trick" gives students practice with column addition.

Tell the students that you and several students are going to write six-digit numbers on the chalkboard. The numbers are then to be added by the members of the class. Unbeknownst to the students, on each of your turns you control the final result and thus can predict the total sum before they even begin to add the numbers.

As each number is written on the chalkboard, have the students copy it on their papers. When all five numbers have been written, each student should add the total to see if your prediction was accurate.

1. On the chalkboard have a student write a six-digit number *that ends in any number other than zero or one.*

2. Ask another student to write a second six-digit number directly beneath the first one. (The zero/one restriction no longer applies.)

3. Now it's your turn! Each digit you write must total 9 when added with the number *directly above it.* (Note numbers with boxes around them in the illustration.)

4. Have another student write a six-digit number beneath yours.

5. Now it's your turn again. Once more each digit you write must total 9 when added with the digit *directly above it.*

6. Tell students to add all of the numbers. But before they begin, tell them what the sum will be!

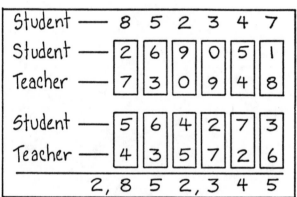

167

(To determine the answer, secretly make the following calculations.)
   a. Put a 2 in front of the original number.
   b. Subtract 2. Voila!

REPRODUCIBLE ACTIVITY PAGE (GRADES 5–6)

Answer Key: Answers will vary.

INSTANT SUMS

Work each step of the magic trick, writing your answers in the space on the right-hand side of the paper.

```
  7  9  4  6  2  5
 [5][3][2][7][4][8]
 [4][6][7][2][5][1]

 [8][7][5][3][9][2]
+[1][2][4][6][0][7]
 2, 7  9  4, 6  2  3
```

When you are sure the magic trick works, try it on someone else. Tell the other person that the two of you will be writing five six-digit numbers. Then you will have the other person add all of the numbers together. But before the person even begins to add, you will tell what the total sum will be.

DIRECTIONS

1. Write a six-digit number that ends with any number *other than zero or one.*

2. Just beneath the first number, write another six-digit number, which may end with any number. (If you are trying this trick with someone else, have the person write both the first and second number. *You* must do STEP 3.)

3. Each number you write must total 9 when mentally added with the number just above it. (Look at the numbers with boxes around them in the illustration at the top of the page.) Write your number.

4. Just below the last number write another six-digit number. (If you are doing this trick with someone else, have the person write this number. *You* must do STEP 5.)

5. Once more each number you write must total 9 when mentally added with the number just above it. Write your number.

6. Add all of the numbers to find the sum.

If you are trying this trick with someone else say, "I am going to have you add all these numbers together. But before you start adding, let me tell you the answer."

To quickly find the answer, do the following:
(1) Put a 2 in front of the very first number.
(2) Subtract 2.

59 142,857 AGAIN?

Materials needed:
½ sheet of lined paper for each student
pencils

[X] reproducible page
[X] total group activity
[ ] individual activity
[ ] partner activity

TOTAL GROUP ACTIVITY

This is a fun way to get your students to practice multiplying by 2, 3, 4, 5, and 6.

Directions:

1. Write the number 142,857 and multiply it by 5. (**Students will discover that they still have the same digits, except the "7" is now in the first position instead of the last position.**)

2. Multiply 142,857 by 4. (**This time the "5" and "7" are the beginning digits rather than the final digits.**)

3. Multiplying 142,857 by 6 will result in the numbers "8, 5, and 7" moving to the beginning position.

4. If 142,857 is multiplied by 2, the last four digits "2, 8, 5, and 7" become the first four digits.

5. To complete the metamorphosis, have students multiply 142,857 by 3. This results in them having the same number they started with, except the "1" that was at the beginning of the number has moved to the end of the number.

REPRODUCIBLE ACTIVITY PAGE (GRADES 5–6)

Answer Key: (1) 714,285, (2) 571,428, (3) 857,142, (4) 285,714, (5) 428,571.

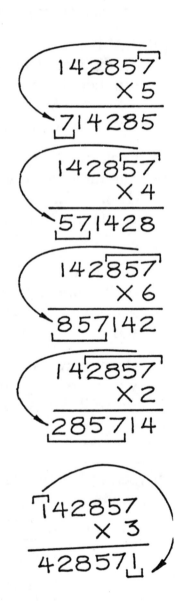

142,857 AGAIN?

Work each step of the magic trick, writing your answers in the space on the right-hand side of the paper.

When you are sure the magic trick works, try it on someone else!

Oh no! I've been moved!

14285

DIRECTIONS

1. Write the number 142857 and multiply it by 5. (When you try this trick with someone else say, "You should have the number you started with, except the 7 at the end of the number has moved to the beginning of the number.")

2. Write 142857 again. Multiply it by 4. (Say: "Now you should have the number you started with, except the 57 at the end of the number has moved to the beginning of the number.")

3. Write 142857 again! Try multiplying it by 6. (Say: "This time the 857 at the end of the number has moved to the beginning position.")

4. Write 142857 one more time and multiply it by 2. (Say: "Now the final 2,857 has moved to the beginning of the number.")

5. For the last trick, multiply 142857 by 3. (Say: "And now you should have the same number you started with, except the 1 at the beginning of the number has moved to the end of the number.")

60   SUM 15 TIC-TAC-TOE

Materials needed:

paper
pencils

☒ reproducible page
☐ total group activity
☐ individual activity
☒ partner activity

PARTNER ACTIVITY

Partners draw a standard tic-tac-toe grid. They decide which person will go first, who will write even numbers (2, 4, 6, 8, 10) during the first game, and who will write odd numbers (1, 3, 5, 7, 9).

Players write their numbers on the paper. Each number may be used only once during a game. As numbers are used, slash marks should be drawn through them.

The students alternate turns, each time writing one of their numbers on the grid. The winner is the first player with 3 in a row, horizontally, vertically, or diagonally, *with a sum of 15.*

Players should alternate between using even and odd numbers. The loser goes first for the next game. The first person to win 5 games is the overall winner.

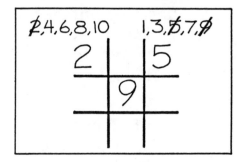

The accompanying reproducible activity page provides an alternate way to explain the game and acquaint students with the basic game format.

REPRODUCIBLE ACTIVITY PAGE (GRADES 2–4)

Answer Key: Answers will vary.

NAME _____

✗✗ 6,8,10 1,3,✗,7✗ SUM 15 TIC-TAC-TOE

For each game one player uses the even numbers, and the other player uses the odd numbers.

Players take turns writing one of the their numbers in the tic-tac-toe squares. As each number is used, an "X" should be written on it. It may not be used again in that game.

The winner is the first person to write three numbers in a row that total 15.

The loser gets to go first for the next game and gets to choose the odd numbers or the even numbers.

Name _____		
ODD NUMBERS		
1, 3, 5, 7, 9		

Name _____		
EVEN NUMBERS		
2, 4, 6, 8, 10		

Name _____		
ODD NUMBERS		
1, 3, 5, 7, 9		

Name _____		
EVEN NUMBERS		
2, 4, 6, 8, 10		

Name _____		
EVEN NUMBERS		
2, 4, 6, 8, 10		

Name _____		
ODD NUMBERS		
1, 3, 5, 7, 9		

61   CIRCLE SUM

Materials needed:

unlined paper
pencils

☒ reproducible page
☐ total group activity
☐ individual activity
☒ partner activity

PARTNER ACTIVITY

This activity provides practice in addition problems that require "carrying."

In order to get the game board ready, one of the players writes the numbers from 7 through 19 at the top of a piece of paper. The other player draws 20 circles on the paper. The players take turns choosing one of the numbers, putting an "X" on it, and then writing it in *two* different circles.

When all circles are filled, there will be three numbers left over. These numbers will not be used in this game.

Players take turns selecting a number, putting an "X" in the corresponding circle and adding the number to their on-going score. The game ends when *both* players reach a total of 100 or more points.

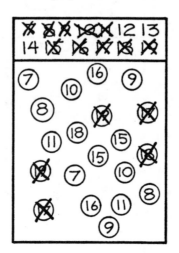

If either player has a score of *exactly* 100, the player earns 3 points. One additional point is awarded to the student who finishes first.

Students begin another game, by drawing 20 new circles and following the above procedures. The first person to win 5 points is the overall winner.

The accompanying reproducible page provides an alternate way to explain the game and acquaint students with the basic game format.

REPRODUCIBLE ACTIVITY PAGE (GRADES 3–5)

Answer Key: Answers will vary.

CIRCLE SUM

Player 1	Player 2
18	19
+17	+17
35	36
	+19
	55

GETTING READY TO PLAY: Players take turns choosing one of the numbers at the top of the GAMEBOARD, putting an "X" on it, and then writing it in *two* different circles.

When all the circles are filled there will be three numbers left over. These numbers will not be used in this game.

PLAYING THE GAME: Players take turns putting an "X" *in a circle* and adding that number to their score. (See the sample above.) The game ends when *both* players have a total of 100 or more points.

SCORING THE GAME: (1) The player who finishes first gets 1 point. (2) If either player has *exactly* 100 points, that player gets 3 extra points.

©1989 by The Center for Applied Research in Education

GAMEBOARD	Player 1.	Player 2.
7, 8, 9, 10, 11, 12, 13, 14, 15, 16, 17, 18, 19	NAME	NAME

62   FIND MY COMPOUND WORD

Materials needed:

☒ reproducible page
☒ total group activity
☐ individual activity
☐ partner activity

TOTAL GROUP ACTIVITY

Begin this activity by reviewing compound words. Then read a sentence from the following list. Tell students the sentence is referring to a compound word. Their challenge is to try to name the word.

Can You Find My Compound Word?

1. This is a small cake. (**cupcake**)
2. You can make shortcake with these. (**strawberries**)
3. You need one of these when you play Pin the Tail on the Donkey. (**blindfold**)
4. This is what you use to steer a bicycle. (**handlebars**)
5. This is part of your finger. (**fingernail**)
6. If you walk this way, you will be very quiet. (**tiptoe**)
7. This place has desks, chairs, students, and a teacher. (**classroom**)
8. Letters are dropped into this when they are ready to be sent. (**mailbox**)
9. You turn this when you want to open a door. (**doorknob**)
10. You might feel this way if you were in a boat during a storm. (**seasick**)
11. These are on your face, just above your eyes. (**eyebrows**)
12. You should put this in your book if you don't want to lose your place. (**bookmark**)
13. You'll need this if you're going out in the rain. (**raincoat**)
14. This is another name for a very bad dream. (**nightmare**)
15. If you don't take care of your teeth, this may be the result. (**toothache**)

REPRODUCIBLE ACTIVITY PAGE (GRADES 2–3)

Answer Key: (**1**) basketball, (**2**) flashlight, (**3**) cookbook, (**4**) broomstick, (**5**) beanstalk, (**6**) bookcase, (**7**) rainbow, (**8**) fireworks, (**9**) grandmother, (**10**) popcorn, (**11**) rattlesnake, (**12**) sand box.

FIND MY COMPOUND WORD

Find a word in the *WORD BANK* that
goes with each clue.

WORD BANK		
broomstick	popcorn	flashlight
rainbow	basketball	beanstalk
fireworks	bookcase	grandmother
sandbox	cookbook	rattlesnake

CLUES

1. You can throw this through a hoop. _____

2. You would like to have one of these
   if you had to go outside in the dark. _____

3. You can find recipes in this. _____

4. A witch needs one of these. _____

5. Jack climbed this. _____

6. This is a place where you can put books. _____

7. You might see this in the sky when it is raining. _____

8. These are fun to watch on the Fourth of July. _____

9. This is your mother's mother. _____

10. It is fun to eat this when you go to the movies. _____

11. You don't want to meet one of these. _____

12. Children like to play in this. _____

63   CAN YOU HEAR ME?

Materials needed:

chalkboard
chalk
eraser

☒ reproducible page
☒ total group activity
☐ individual activity
☐ partner activity

TOTAL GROUP ACTIVITY

Name a letter of the alphabet from one of the following lists and specify where the students are to listen for the sound of the letter, at the beginning, middle, or end of words.

Then slowly read a pair of words from the list. Repeat the words and have the students say them with you. Pause, then say, "Show me." If both words have the letter in the specified position, students should point both of their thumbs up. If both words do not have the letter in the correct position, they should point their thumbs down.

Tell the correct answer and then read the next word pair.

Variation

If the students look around to see what the others have done before giving their own hand signals, have them do the activity with their eyes closed. After they have signaled each response, tell them the correct answer.

Activity Lists

Can you hear "N" at the beginning of these words?

1. need, never (**yes**)
2. need, spin (**no**)
3. need, number (**yes**)
4. need, name (**yes**)
5. need, men (**no**)
6. need, noise (**yes**)
7. need, train (**no**)
8. need, nickel (**yes**)
9. need, can (**no**)
10. need, night (**yes**)

Can you hear "N" at the end of both of these words?

1. rain, fan (**yes**)
2. rain, minute (**no**)
3. rain, done (**yes**)
4. rain, name (**no**)
5. rain, plan (**yes**)
6. rain, again (**yes**)
7. rain, green (**yes**)
8. rain, nurse (**no**)
9. rain, ribbon (**yes**)
10. rain, nut (**no**)

Can you hear "N" in the middle of both of these words?

1. finish, dinner (**yes**)
2. finish, minute (**yes**)
3. finish, phone (**no**)
4. finish, net (**no**)
5. finish, cannot (**yes**)
6. finish, pony (**yes**)
7. finish, one (**no**)
8. finish, run (**no**)
9. finish, gentle (**yes**)
10. finish, connect (**yes**)

Can you hear "B" at the beginning of both of these words?

1. ball, bicycle (**yes**)
2. ball, bird (**yes**)
3. ball, above (**no**)
4. ball, able (**no**)
5. ball, beautiful (**yes**)
6. ball, basket (**yes**)
7. ball, pebble (**no**)
8. ball, birthday (**yes**)
9. ball, bang (**yes**)
10. ball, cab (**no**)

Can you hear "B" at the end of both of these words?

1. job, crib (**yes**)
2. job, robot (**no**)
3. job, tub (**yes**)
4. job, bear (**no**)
5. job, web (**yes**)
6. job, bend (**no**)
7. job, robe (**yes**)
8. job, box (**no**)
9. job, grab (**yes**)
10. job, rub (**yes**)

Can you hear "B" in the middle of both of these words?

1. rabbit, ribbon (**yes**)
2. rabbit, cabbage (**yes**)
3. rabbit, bitten (**no**)
4. rabbit, habit (**yes**)
5. rabbit, robin (**yes**)
6. rabbit, beetle (**no**)
7. rabbit, pebble (**yes**)
8. rabbit, bitten (**no**)
9. rabbit, rubber (**yes**)
10. rabbit, balloon (**no**)

Can you hear "R" at the beginning of both of these words?

1. rain, river (**yes**)
2. rain, roof (**yes**)
3. rain, berry (**no**)
4. rain, rainbow (**yes**)
5. rain, rhyme (**yes**)
6. rain, far (**no**)
7. rain, ready (**yes**)
8. rain, hurry (**no**)
9. rain, more (**no**)
10. rain, radish (**yes**)

Can you hear "R" at the end of both of these words?

1. scare, steer (**yes**)
2. scare, rabbit (**no**)
3. scare, clear (**yes**)
4. scare, arrow (**no**)
5. scare, bear (**yes**)
6. scare, around (**no**)
7. scare, rest (**no**)
8. scare, already (**no**)
9. scare, tear (**yes**)
10. scare, sore (**yes**)

Can you hear "R" in the middle of both of these words?

1. berry, giraffe (**yes**)
2. berry, roll (**no**)
3. berry, carrot (**yes**)
4. berry, ruffle (**no**)
5. berry, ready (**no**)
6. berry, parade (**yes**)
7. berry, parrot (**yes**)
8. berry, robin (**no**)
9. berry, sparrow (**yes**)
10. berry, roof (**no**)

REPRODUCIBLE ACTIVITY PAGE (GRADES 1–2)

Answer Key: *Circled Words*—mouse, mother, mine, mad, mail, make, milk, map; *Boxed Words*—time, some, drum, room, come, hum. Students' designs will vary.

CAN YOU HEAR ME?

Make an orange ring around all words that start with an "m" sound.

Make a green box around all words that end with an "m" sound.

mouse   mother   mine

time   some

drum

mad   mail

room

come   hum

make   milk   map

Take your orange crayon. Make a design by connecting the orange rings.

Take your green crayon. Make a design by connecting the green boxes.

64 SHIFTING LETTERS

Materials needed:

chalkboard
chalk
eraser

☒ reproducible page
☒ total group activity
☐ individual activity
☐ partner activity

TOTAL GROUP ACTIVITY

On the chalkboard write a word from the following list. Have the students mentally substitute one letter to form a new word. The initial letter, vowel, or final letter may be changed.

Call on a student to write his or her word and draw a box around the letter that was changed. Then have this student choose a volunteer to go to the chalkboard. This person must substitute one letter in the previous student's word to form a new word, which is written on the chalkboard. Play continues in this manner, until students can think of no additional words.

Challenge students to see how long a list they can make *without repeating any words.*

Change One Letter to Make a New Word

fun	rag	pet	mad
lap	top	lid	sun
pen	bug	dot	

man
ma**t**
m**e**t
bet
be**g**
leg
l**o**g
hog
ho**t**
h**i**t
hi**d**

REPRODUCIBLE ACTIVITY PAGE (GRADES 1–3)

Answer Key: Answers will vary.

SHIFTING LETTERS

Change *one* letter in the first word.

Write the new word and make a box around the letter that was changed.

Keep writing new words, each time changing one letter. No word may be repeated within the same list.

How long a list can you make?

hog
l[o]g
le[g]
le[t]
[me]t
me[n]
[p]en

man	mop	sun	hid
m[e]n			
[p]en			

©1989 by The Center for Applied Research in Education

65   SPELL MY WORD

Materials needed:

chalkboard
chalk
eraser
¼ sheet of paper for each student
pencils

☒ reproducible page
☒ total group activity
☐ individual activity
☐ partner activity

TOTAL GROUP ACTIVITY

Second and third grade students write a four- or five-letter word on their papers. Older students should write a five- to eight-letter word.

Choose a student to come to the chalkboard and write the first and last letter of his or her word and a dash for each omitted letter.

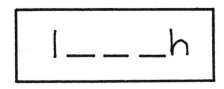

The other students try to guess the word. If it has not been identified within three guesses, have the student give a clue: "You do this when something is funny."

The person who guesses the word must also identify the missing letters, or the turn passes to another student. The one who answers correctly gets to write the next "mystery word" on the chalkboard.

REPRODUCIBLE ACTIVITY PAGE (GRADES 2–4)

Staple completed reproducible pages into a class puzzle book to be used individually or as a total group activity.

Answer Key: Clues and answers will vary.

SPELL MY WORD

Think of a word and a clue that goes with the word. Write the clue. Draw a line for each letter in the word. Then write the first and last letter of the word. (See the example at the top of the page.)

CLUE: _____

WORD: _

CLUE: _____

WORD: _

CLUE: _____

WORD: _

CLUE: _____

WORD: _

CLUE: _____

WORD: _

CLUE: _____

WORD: _

66 DON'T SAY THAT VOWEL!

Materials needed:

TOTAL GROUP ACTIVITY

Students name items within categories, but each category has a vowel restriction placed on it. For instance, when naming animals, the words cannot have an "o." Because of the elimination of certain vowels, this activity is trickier than it first appears! (Sample answers are given below.)

PARTNER ADAPTATION (GRADES 2–3)

Materials needed:

lined paper
pencils
optional: Don't Say That Vowel! reproducible activity page, one for each partner

Give partners the accompanying reproducible page, or assign them a category and vowel restriction. (See suggestion below.) The partners work together to solve the activity.

Animals, *with No "O"s*	*Kitchen Items,* *with No "A"s*
cat	stove
mice	pots
zebra	skillet
chicken	towel
duck	dish cloth
giraffe	spoon
elephant	fork
seal	knife
turkey	counter
tiger	shelves
penguin	dishes
cattle	tongs
sheep	sink

Things that Make Sounds, with No "E"s

bird
lion
duck
cow
car
fog horn
train
baby
crowd
cat
dog
crow
boat

Fruits/Vegetables, with No "O"s

grapefruit
apple
pear
peach
lettuce
celery
squash
cabbage
beans
peas
beets
cucumber
radish
grapes
plums
strawberry

Colors, with No "A"s

blue	violet
green	pink
brown	indigo
red	grey
yellow	
turquoise	
purple	
white	

Moving on Land or Water, with No "I"s

roller skate	jet
plane	bus
car	trolley
canoe	subway
rowboat	
tugboat	
scooter	
motorcycle	
moped	
skateboard	
barge	
wagon	

Types of Jobs, with No "I"s

plumber	stewardess
carpenter	lawyer
teacher	banker
doctor	farmer
secretary	photographer
nurse	forest ranger
clerk	accountant
salesperson	

Inside a House, with No "E"s

(Note: When the letter "e" is omitted, many words are eliminated; therefore, this category should be quite broad, including clothing, etc.)

chair
couch
lamp
rug
coat
mirror
hat
plants
books
scissors
curtains
hairbrush
comb
toothbrush
shampoo
bathtub

REPRODUCIBLE ACTIVITY PAGE (GRADES 2–6)

Answer Key: Answers will vary.

Suggestion: If you do not have time to duplicate the reproducible page, as an alternate procedure assign one or more of the categories and vowel restrictions given. Students should write as many words as they can think of for each category.

DON'T SAY THAT VOWEL!

Look at the charts below. Each category has a vowel restriction placed on it. For instance, when naming animals, the words may not have the letter "o" in them.

You are to write as many words as you can think of that follow the rule and fit within the category. This activity is trickier than it first appears. Watch out!

ANIMALS, WITH NO "O"s
cat

COLORS, WITH NO "A"s

FRUITS/VEGETABLES WITH NO "O"s

THINGS THAT MAKE SOUNDS WITH NO "E"s

67   TIRED OLD WORDS

Materials needed:

chalkboard
chalk
eraser

☒ reproducible page
☒ total group activity
☐ individual activity
☐ partner activity

TOTAL GROUP ACTIVITY

Have students think of words to replace an overused (tired old) word: good, bad, went, etc. Write ten to fifteen of their words on the chalkboard, or write one of the groups of words listed below. Call on a volunteer to use the "tired old" word in a sentence.

Example: When I saw I had all "A"s on my report card, I *went* home.

The student calls on a classmate to repeat the sentence, replacing the tired old word with one of the words listed on the chalkboard.

Example: When I saw I had all "A"s on my report card, I *dashed* home.

Encourage students to think of sentences that "beg" for a specific descriptive word.

Example: The snake went through the grass. (slithered)

As each word is used, place a check mark by it, and explain that no word may be used more than twice.

Went (How People Move)		*Said*	
crawl	race	groaned	mumbled
hurry	creep	shouted	grumbled
stagger	dash	cried	squealed
tiptoe	stumble	whined	giggled
rush	saunter	whispered	wondered
stroll	waddle	gasped	asked
trudge	limp	moaned	replied
amble		growled	

Went (How Animals Move)

glide	flutter
gallop	climb
amble	trot
bounce	crawl
dart	slither
scamper	
bound	
skim	
hover	
soar	

Good/Bad (How People Feel)

excited	cozy
angry	delighted
smug	uncomfortable
proud	miserable
worried	
wretched	
desperate	
confident	
exhilerated	
relieved	

Big

huge	large
tall	bulky
tremendous	immense
enormous	massive
gigantic	imposing
towering	

REPRODUCIBLE ACTIVITY PAGE (GRADES 3–6)

Answer Key: Answers will vary. Accept any that seem appropriate. If there is time, have students discuss their answers and let them share the sentences they wrote.

NAME_____

TIRED OLD WORDS

Find a word in the box to take the place of the words in italics. Each word may be used only once.

SET A

trudged	limped	crept
ambled	stumbled	dashed

1. I *walked* home after I sprained my ankle. _____

2. When he heard the good news, he *ran* home. _____

3. He *walked* into the house, hoping no one would hear him. _____

4. Slowly we *walked* up the steep hill. _____

5. The two old men talked about their childhood as they *walked* across the field.

_____

Write a sentence using the leftover word. _____

SET B

grumbled	groaned	wondered
gasped	squealed	whispered

1. "I feel awful," she *said.* _____

2. "How much longer will I have to sit

here?" *thought* the little boy. _____

3. "Oh this is just what I wanted for

my birthday," *said* Sally. _____

4. "Promise me you won't tell anyone

about this," *said* Betsy. _____

5. "I think there's a burglar outside,"

said Willie. _____

Write a sentence using the leftover word. _____

_____

68   SYNONYMS WITH STYLE

Materials needed:

☒ reproducible page
☒ total group activity
☒ individual activity
☐ partner activity

TOTAL GROUP ACTIVITY

Write numerals 1 through 25 on the chalkboard. Explain that you have a list of words numbered from 1 to 25. The higher the number the more difficult the word. Call on a student to choose a number. Read the corresponding word from your list. The student should replace the word with a more "stylish" one. For instance, instead of *sweat*, they might say *perspiration*. If a student cannot think of an acceptable synonym, call on others until an answer is found.

This method allows students to choose an easy word or the challenge of a more difficult one. As each numeral is used, erase it from the chalkboard, so that repetitions are avoided.

ADAPTATION FOR AN INDIVIDUAL STUDENT (GRADES 3–6)

Materials needed:
¼ sheets of lined paper
pencils

Have the student list a simple word, and its "stylish" companions on a ¼ sheet of lined paper. (This is an excellent way to encourage a student to pay close attention to words that are used in both spoken and written language.) Designate a place for these to be handed in. When sufficient words have been collected, sequence and number them from easy to difficult. Then use the list for a total group activity.

1. finish (**complete**)
2. right (**correct**)
3. ask (**request**)
4. dirty (**soiled**)
5. old (**ancient, elderly**)
6. fix (**repair**)
7. mad (**angry**)
8. find (**locate**)
9. argue (**quarrel**)
10. hurt (**injure**)
11. help (**aid, assist**)
12. catch (**capture**)
13. late (**tardy**)
14. rude (**impolite**)
15. get (**obtain**)
16. beg (**plead, coax**)

17. tired (**exhausted**)
18. ask (**inquire**)
19. handy (**useful**)
20. stop (**cease**)
21. small (**tiny, minute**)
22. interesting (**fascinating, intriguing**)
23. show (**demonstrate**)
24. hold (**grasp**)

25. sleepy (**drowsy, lethargic**)
26. ate (**devoured, consumed**)
27. empty (**deserted, vacant**)
28. disappear (**vanish**)
29. hard (**difficult, complicated**)
30. mix (**combine, blend**)
31. hide (**conceal**)
32. blame (**accuse**)

REPRODUCIBLE ACTIVITY PAGE (GRADES 3–6)

Answer Key: Sample answers follow but all synonyms should be accepted. (1) enormous, huge, gigantic; (2) amusing, humorous, comical; (3) horrible, terrible, dreadful; (4) dislike, despise, detest, loathe; (5) intelligent, brilliant, bright, wise; (6) dull, uninteresting, dreary; (7) hastily, hurriedly; (8) moist, damp, soaked, drenched; (9) frightened, terrified; (10) glanced, gazed, stared, peered; (11) considerate, thoughtful; (12) shrieked, screamed; (13) courageous, bold, fearless; (14) bitter, tart.

NAME _____

SYNONYMS WITH STYLE

Write two synonyms for each word listed
below. A dictionary or thesaurus will help you
find synonyms that have "real style."

1. big _____ _____

2. funny _____ _____

3. awful _____ _____

4. hate _____ _____

5. smart _____ _____

6. boring _____ _____

7. quickly _____ _____

8. wet _____ _____

9. scared _____ _____

10. looked _____ _____

11. kind _____ _____

12. yell _____ _____

13. brave _____ _____

14. sour _____ _____

69   GUESS MY WORD

Materials needed:

☐ reproducible page
☒ total group activity
☐ individual activity
☐ partner activity

TOTAL GROUP ACTIVITY

Tell students that you have a list of words, each of which begins with a _____ (name the specific letter of the alphabet). Challenge them to discover the mystery words by listening to your clues.

Words That Begin With "B"

1. A place to keep money. (**bank**)
2. The outside part of a tree. (**bark**)
3. A building where farm animals are kept. (**barn**)
4. A person who cuts hair. (**barber**)
5. The part of a knife that is used to cut. (**blade**)
6. An animal that flies at night and often lives in caves. (**bat**)
7. This keeps you warm in bed. (**blanket**)
8. A severe storm with wind and snow. (**blizzard**)
9. The first meal of the day. (**breakfast**)
10. This is a word that describes a man who lacks hair on his head. (**bald**)

Words That Begin With "T"

1. An instrument that is used to measure temperature. (**thermometer**)
2. This animal doesn't like Thanksgiving. (**turkey**)
3. A red light mounted on the back of a car. (**taillight**)
4. A person who makes, repairs, and alters clothing. (**tailor**)
5. The opposite of wild. (**tame**)
6. This animal beat the hare in a race. (**tortoise**)
7. This animal turns into a frog or a toad. (**tadpole**)
8. When you look through it, things that are far away look closer. (**telescope**)
9. This tiny insect can eat wood and destroy a house. (**termite**)
10. The part of the leg between the knee and hip. (**thigh**)

Words That Begin With "R"

1. A place to eat. (**restaurant**)
2. You use this to tie around a present. (**ribbon**)
3. Animals that are cold blooded. (**reptiles**)
4. The top of a building. (**roof**)
5. A male chicken. (**rooster**)
6. An animal that looks like it has a mask on its face. (**raccoon**)
7. A straight piece of wood that is used to measure. (**ruler**)
8. A torn or worn piece of cloth. (**rag**)
9. The opposite of fake. (**real**)
10. This is what you see when you look in a mirror. (**reflection**)

Words That Begin With "L"

1. The sound you make when you see or hear something funny. (**laugh**)
2. A cover that fits on a pot or pan. (**lid**)
3. A flash of electricity in the sky. (**lightning**)
4. The painted mark that is used to show the center of a road. (**line**)
5. A small red beetle that has black spots. (**ladybug**)
6. A room or building where books are kept. (**library**)
7. A green leafy vegetable that is used in salads. (**lettuce**)
8. A light that can be carried. (**lantern**)
9. Something that holds windows and doors so they cannot be opened. (**lock**)
10. A special kind of candy that is black in color. (**licorice**)

Words That Begin With "H"

1. A main road for cars. (**highway**)
2. An animal's skin. (**hide**)
3. If a group of animals live together, this is what the group is called. (**herd**)
4. A device placed over the ears to listen to music. (**headphones**)
5. The floor of a fireplace. (**hearth**)
6. An animal that is somewhat like a mouse, but larger. (**hamster**)
7. The part that is used to steer a bicycle. (**handlebars**)
8. A house for bees to live in. (**hive**)
9. A hanging bed, often tied between two trees. (**hammock**)
10. The back part of your foot. (**heel**)

Words That Begin With "F"

1. One part of a fish's body that helps it swim. (**fin**)
2. If you're going to take pictures with your camera, you'll need this. (**film**)
3. You can see these on the Fourth of July. (**fireworks**)
4. This is nice to have if the electricity goes off. (**flashlight**)
5. A small animal that leaps and lives near water. (**frog**)
6. You leave these on the sidewalk after you walk through water. (**footprints**)
7. A special type of boat that is used to carry people and cars. (**ferry**)
8. You make this when you close your hand tightly. (**fist**)
9. A story that teaches a lesson. (**fable**)
10. A building where things are manufactured. (**factory**)

70   CONTEXT CLUES

Materials needed:

☐ reproducible page
☒ total group activity
☐ individual activity
☐ partner activity

TOTAL GROUP ACTIVITY

Read a sentence from the following list and ask students to define the word in italics. Explain that by listening to how a word is used in a sentence, they will often be able to discover the meaning of an unfamiliar word. After each word is defined, ask for a volunteer to use it in a sentence.

What Does This Word Mean?

1. We couldn't eat the fruit because it was *spoiled. Spoiled* means _____. **(not good)**
2. Much damage was done by the *great* storm. *Great* means _____. **(large)**
3. The clothes in the dryer are still *damp. Damp* means _____. **(wet)**
4. Is it *chilly* outside: *Chilly* means _____. **(cool)**
5. I'm going to help Dad *haul* all this junk to the dump. *Haul means* _____. **(take)**
6. She always seems so *cheerful. Cheerful* means _____. **(happy)**
7. The writing was so *faint* I could hardly read it. *Faint* means _____. **(not easily seen)**
8. The fawn was so *still*, I didn't even see him. *Still* means _____. **(quiet)**
9. The *rim* of the vase was chipped. *Rim* means _____. **(edge)**
10. The *ancient* building was still standing. *Ancient* means _____. **(old)**
11. Was your dad *annoyed* when you came home late? *Annoyed* means _____. **(angry)**
12. Please *dim* the lights. *Dim* means _____. **(turn down)**
13. The way the dog walked through the room was very *comical. Comical* means _____. **(funny)**
14. What was his *reply* to your question? *Reply* means _____. **(answer)**
15. As we *approached* the house, I got more and more excited. *Approached* means _____. **(came to)**
16. The man *demanded* an answer to his question. *Demanded* means _____. **(asked for)**
17. That is a very *attractive* flower arrangement. *Attractive* means _____. **(beautiful)**
18. Have they *captured* the lion yet? *Captured* means _____. **(caught)**
19. I get tired of *toting* home my books every night. *Toting* means _____. **(carrying)**
20. He *seized* the gun from the robber's hand. *Seized* means _____. **(grabbed)**
21. I *chatted* with my friend after school. *Chatted* means _____. **(talked)**

22. The man tried to *conceal* the stolen ring. *Conceal* means _____. **(hide)**

23. The teacher said, "There is too much *commotion* in the room." *Commotion* means _____. **(noise, disruption)**

24. The *vacant* classroom looked strange. *Vacant* means _____. **(empty)**

25. After their long *journey*, they were very tired. *Journey* means _____. **(trip)**

26. The children were *flustered* by the change in plans. *Flustered* means _____. **(confused)**

27. *Approximately* 100 people came to see the play. *Approximately* means _____. **(nearly)**

28. The clever fox *flattered* the bear with his comments. *Flattered* means _____. **(said nice things)**

29. Dad told us about his *comrades* in the army. *Comrades* means _____. **(friends)**

30. Did you see the tree *sway* during the storm? *Sway* means _____. **(move from side to side)**

31. The antelope is a very *swift* animal. *Swift* means _____. **(fast)**

32. The *terrified* cat ran into the house. *Terrified* means _____. **(frightened)**

33. The teacher waited for the class to *respond*. *Respond* means _____. **(answer)**

34. Mom told us an *amusing* story during dinner. *Amusing* means _____. **(funny)**

35. After the long hike they were *exhausted*. *Exhausted* means _____. **(very tired)**

36. Frank was the first one to find the *solution* to the puzzle. *Solution* means _____. **(answer)**

37. Kelly and I tried to *coax* the kitten to come out from under the house. *Coax* means _____. **(persuade)**

38. Why did he *refuse* to go? *Refuse* means _____. **(to say no)**

39. Janet decided to try to *assemble* the model by herself. *Assemble* means _____. **(put together)**

40. It was a *dreadful* situation. *Dreadful* means _____. **(awful)**

41. The *cautious* kitten tiptoed across the wet floor. *Cautious* means _____. **(careful)**

42. Dad asked me to *fetch* some wood for the fireplace. *Fetch* means _____. **(bring)**

43. It wasn't much fun being around the *cranky* child. *Cranky* means _____. **(fussy, unpleasant)**

44. Mrs. Jacobson said she would *demonstrate* how to do the math problem. *Demonstrate* means _____. **(show)**

45. Everyone was *astonished* by the answer. *Astonished* means _____. **(surprised)**

46. I *loathe* spinach. *Loathe* means _____. **(dislike, hate)**

47. The man *ambled* down the street as if nothing had happened. *Ambled* means _____. **(walked)**

48. The doctor said an *arid* climate would be good for his health. *Arid* means _____. **(dry)**

49. The *catastrophic* storm caused many injuries. *Catastrophic* means _____. **(terrible)**

50. It is difficult to imagine the *vast* space between planets. *Vast* means _____. **(huge)**

51. The sailors made a *gallant* effort to save their ship. *Gallant* means _____. **(heroic)**

52. Are they really going to *demolish* that building? *Demolish* means _____. **(wreck)**

53. I do not want to go in that *dingy* little restaurant. *Dingy* means _____. (dirty)

54. The captain told the soldiers to *cease* their fire. *Cease* means _____. (stop)

55. I wonder what they will *elect* to do. *Elect* means _____. (choose)

56. The tall buildings *loomed* in the distance. *Loomed* means _____. (appeared)

57. Ginny said the old dock was *hazardous*. *Hazardous* means _____. (dangerous)

58. The lost puppy looked up with a *woebegone* expression. *Woebegone* means _____. (sad)

59. Where does that river *originate*? *Originate* means _____. (begin)

60. As they walked along the edge of the cliff, they realized they were in a *precarious* situation. *Precarious* means _____. (unsafe)

61. The longer he talked, the more *exasperated* I became. *Exasperated* means _____. (annoyed)

62. A *muffled* sound came from the box. *Muffled* means _____. (faint)

63. You should have seem him *devour* the cookies! *Devour* means _____. (eat up greedily)

64. When they heard the news they were *jubilant*. *Jubilant* means _____. (happy)

65. His *anecdote* made everyone laugh. *Anecdote* means (amusing or interesting story)

71 THE WORD KEEPS CHANGING!

Materials needed:

☒ reproducible page
☒ total group activity
☐ individual activity
☐ partner activity

TOTAL GROUP ACTIVITY

Read the following sentences and have students suggest possible "missing words" that start with the letter you designate. Students should try to supply colorful responses as often as possible. Sample responses are given in parentheses, but all logical answers should be accepted.

What Words Could Fill the Blanks?

1. When Kenneth looked at the _____ tree, he couldn't believe his eyes.

   A. The word starts with *h.* (**huge**)
   B. The word starts with *e.* (**enormous**)
   C. The word begins with *g.* (**gigantic**)
   D. The word begins with *t.* (**towering, tall**)

2. The old man was very _____.

   A. The word starts with *b.* (**bright, brilliant**)
   B. The word starts with *w.* (**wise**)
   C. The word begins with *g.* (**grouchy**)
   D. The word begins with *f.* (**forgetful**)

3. It was a _____ day.

   A. The word starts with *w.* (**wonderful, windy**)
   B. The word starts with *c.* (**cloudy, clear**)
   C. The word begins with *t.* (**tiring, terrible**)
   D. The word begins with *s.* (**stormy**)

4. I couldn't believe how _____ the water was.

   A. The word starts with *c.* (**clear**)
   B. The word starts with *m.* (**muddy, murky**)
   C. The word begins with *w.* (**warm**)
   D. The word begins with *r.* (**rough**)

5. The water _____ down the hill.

   A. The word starts with *g*. (**gushed, gurgled**)

   B. The word starts with *t*. (**trickled, tumbled**)

   C. The word begins with *s*. (**splashed**)

   D. The word begins with *r*. (**rushed**)

6. The goat _____ up the hill.

   A. The word starts with *s*. (**scampered**)

   B. The word starts with *t*. (**trotted**)

   C. The word begins with *b*. (**bounded**)

   D. The word begins with *d*. (**darted**)

7. I thought that movie was _____.

   A. The word starts with *h*. (**horrible, hilarious, horrifying**)

   B. The word starts with *f*. (**fantastic**)

   C. The word begins with *e*. (**exciting, enjoyable**)

   D. The word begins with *s*. (**superb, splendid**)

8. We climbed the _____ mountain.

   A. The word starts with *r*. (**rocky**)

   B. The word starts with *s*. (**steep**)

   C. The word begins with *j*. (**jagged**)

   D. The word begins with *t*. (**towering**)

9. Our teacher said it was important to make _____ measurements.

   A. The word starts with *c*. (**careful, correct**)

   B. The word starts with *e*. (**exact**)

   C. The word begins with *p*. (**precise**)

   D. The word begins with *a*. (**accurate**)

10. My grandmother sat in the chair looking very _____.

   A. The word starts with *w*. (**worried**)

   B. The word starts with *p*. (**peaceful, perplexed**)

   C. The word begins with *r*. (**relaxed**)

   D. The word begins with *c*. (**confused, concerned**)

REPRODUCIBLE ACTIVITY PAGE (GRADES 4–6)

Answer Key: Answers will vary. Sample answers follow. (1) neat; immaculate; tidy; spotless or spic and span; (2) conscientious, careless, clever, or considerate; polite or pleasant; intelligent; thoughtful or tactful; (3) hungry; shivering, scared, or starving; whining, or whimpering; frightened or friendly; (4) excited; surprised or startled; nervous; flustered or flabbergasted.

THE WORD KEEPS CHANGING!

Read the sentences below and think of four *interesting words* that could fill the blanks. But watch out! Each word must begin with a certain letter. A thesaurus will help you discover a variety of possible words to go with each sentence.

1. Janet always kept her room _____.
Write a word that starts with:

n _____   t _____

i _____   s _____

2. Mrs. Jackson was a very _____ person.
Write a word that starts with:

c _____   i _____

p _____   t _____

3. I found a _____ puppy on my doorstep last night.
Write a word that starts with:

h _____   w_____

s _____   f _____

4. I was so _____ I couldn't say a word.
Write a word that starts with:

e _____   n _____

s _____   f _____

72   ANIMAL SPECIFIC VOCABULARY

Materials needed:

chalkboard
chalk
eraser

☒ reproducible page
☒ total group activity
☐ individual activity
☐ partner activity

TOTAL GROUP ACTIVITY

Draw a chart on the chalkboard listing animals in a column on the left. Label four columns across the top of the chart: *group, male, female,* and *offspring.*

Name one of the animals on the chart. Then ask if anyone can tell you either what group it belongs to, or its female, male, or offspring label. For example:

whale: group, pod
female, cow
male, bull
young, calf

When a correct answer is given, write the response on the chart in the proper location and have the student call on a volunteer to provide another one of the missing pieces of information.

If students are unable to complete the chart, fill in the missing words and discuss the answers. This fascinates students because many of the names are complete surprises!

REPRODUCIBLE ACTIVITY PAGE (GRADES 4–6)

This makes an excellent partner or small group project. Plan to allow time for students to go to the library to locate information that is missing on their charts.

Answer Key: CHICKEN—flock, cock, hen, chick; DEER—herd, buck, doe, fawn; LION—pride, lion, lioness, cub; GOOSE—skein or gaggle, gander, goose, gosling; GOAT—flock, billy, nanny, kid; TIGER—(no group name), tiger, tigress, cub; HORSE—herd, stallion, mare, colt (male) or filly (female) or foal (baby); SHEEP—flock, ram, ewe, lamb; WHALE—pod, bull, cow, calf; ELEPHANT—herd, bull, cow, calf; DUCK—flock or skein, drake, duck, duckling; FOX—pack, fox, vixen, cub; FISH—school or shoal, fish, fish, fry or fingerling; PIG—herd, boar, sow, piglet or pigling; TURKEY—rafter, cock, hen, chick.

NAME _____

ANIMAL SPECIFIC VOCABULARY

How many spaces can you fill in?

ANIMAL(S)	GROUP	MALE	FEMALE	OFFSPRING
cattle	herd	bull	cow	calf
chicken				
deer				
lion				
goose				
goat				
tiger				
horse				
sheep				
whale				
elephant				
duck				
fox				
fish				
pig				
turkey				

73 SO THAT'S MY STEM!

Materials needed:

chalkboard
chalk
eraser

☒ reproducible page
☒ total group activity
☐ individual activity
☐ partner activity

TOTAL GROUP ACTIVITY

Explain that some English words derive from Greek and Latin. Therefore, knowledge of the more common stems is extremely helpful in determining the meaning of unfamiliar words. This activity acquaints students with some of these stems and provides practice in using them.

Following are seven sets of questions to be read to the class. Each set helps the students discover and use one particular word stem.

Word Derivatives

1. A *telegraph* is a written message, sent by electrical impulses. (**Write graph on the chalkboard.**)

    An *autograph* is a person's written name.

    What do you think *graph* means? (**something that writes, draws, or records, or something written, drawn, or recorded**)

    What do these words mean?

    phonograph (**a machine that reproduces sound from a record**)

    seismograph (**an instrument that measures and makes a written record of the location and strength of an earthquake**)

    photograph (**a way of recording a picture**)

2. A *monocle* is an eyeglass for only one eye. (**Write *mono* on the chalkboard.**)

    Monogamy is the custom of marrying only one person at a time.

    What do you think *mono* means? (**one, single**)

    What do these words mean?

    monorail (**a railway in which the track consists of only one rail**)

    monotone (**a series of words or sounds uttered on a single tone**)

    monoplane (**a plane with one set of wings**)

3. An *octuple* is something that has eight parts or eight copies. (**Write *octo* and *octa* on the chalkboard.**)

    An *octopus* is a marine animal that has eight legs.

    What do you think *octo* or *octa* mean? (**eight**)

What do these words mean?

octahedron (a three-dimensional figure that has eight surfaces or faces)

octet (any group of eight, such as eight singers)

octogenarian (a person who is eighty to eighty-nine years old)

4. *Malice* means that someone would like to harm others. (**Write *mal* on the chalkboard.**)

A *malady* is a bad illness.

What do you think *mal* means? (**bad**)

What do these words mean?

maltreated (treatly badly)

maladjustment (a bad or faulty fit)

malign (to say bad things about someone)

5. An *intercom* is a system used to communicate between rooms. (**Write *inter* on the chalkboard.**)

An *interval* is a space between two objects or between two periods of time.

What do you think *inter* means? (**between**)

What do these words mean?

interfere (to come between the affairs of others)

intergalactic (between galaxies)

interim (an interval of time between two events or two periods)

6. *Superior* means far above average. (**Write *super* on the chalkboard.**)

Superfluous means more than what is required or needed.

What do you think *super* means? (**more, over, beyond, above**)

What do these words mean?

supersonic (over and above the speed of sound)

superabundant (more than ample)

supercharge (increase the power of an engine)

7. *Manacles* are metal rings used for holding someone's hands together, such as handcuffs. (**Write *mana* on the chalkboard.**)

A *manicure* consists of shaping, cleaning, and polishing the nails on a person's hands.

What do you think *mana* means? (**hand**)

What do these words mean?

manuscript (book or other writing done by hand)

manipulate (to control by skilled use of the hands)

manual (handbook; anything that is done by the hands or used by the hands, such as manual labor or manual controls)

REPRODUCIBLE ACTIVITY PAGE (GRADES 5–6)

Answer Key: The wording of answers will vary. Sample answers follow. (1) water; producing electricity by using water; a seaplane, also a boat that skims over the surface of the water at high speeds; growing plants in water containing nutrients, rather than in soil; (2) heat; relating to hot water, such as hot springs; electricity made by the flow of heat; an engine operated by heat; (3) water; a tank filled with water in which animals and plants are kept; a structure or canal designed to move water; a person trained to swim in the water.

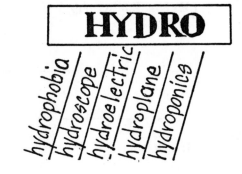

SO THAT'S MY STEM!

Many words in the English language come from Greek and Latin words. The Greek and Latin words are called stems.

Below are three sets of questions. Each set will help you discover and use one word stem.

1. *Hydrophobia* is a fear of water.
   A *hydroscope* is a device used to see under water.

   What do you think *hydro* means? _____
   What do these words mean?

   hydroelectric _____

   hydroplane _____

   hydroponics _____

2. A *thermostat* is a device used to control temperature.
   A *thermometer* is an instrument for measuring temperature.

   What do you think *thermo* means? _____
   What do these words mean?

   hydrothermal _____

   thermoelectricity _____

   thermomotor _____

3. An *aquaplane* is a board on which a person rides in a standing position as it is pulled through the water by a motorboat.
   Something that is *aquatic* lives or grows in water.

   What do you think *aqua* or *aque* means? _____
   What do these words mean?

   aquarium _____

   aqueduct _____

   aquanaut _____

74   NOUN PAIRS

Materials needed:

☐ reproducible page
☒ total group activity
☐ individual activity
☐ partner activity

TOTAL GROUP ACTIVITY

Review nouns with students, making certain they know that nouns name a person, place, or object.

From the following list read a pair of words twice; pause to give students time to think. They should respond on the signal, "Show me," by raising their arms in the air if both are nouns, or crossing their arms on their chests if one is a verb (mismatch).

Variation

Materials needed:

lined paper for each student
pencils

Have students number their papers from 1 to 25. Read each pair of words. Students write "N" if both words are nouns or "X" if they are a mismatch.

Are These Words Noun Pairs?

1. aquarium, escalator (**match**)
2. bake, mosquito (**mismatch—bake**)
3. playground, flashlight (**match**)
4. acrobat, breathe (**mismatch—breathe**)
5. medicine, birthday (**match**)
6. baker, supermarket (**match**)

7. bury, hospital (**mismatch—bury**)
8. octopus, introduce (**mismatch—introduce**)
9. pebble, parent (**match**)
10. California, teacher (**match**)
11. enter, theater (**mismatch—enter**)
12. child, library (**match**)
13. television, argue (**mismatch—argue**)
14. factory, alphabet (**match**)
15. recycle, scientist (**mismatch—recycle**)
16. restaurant, dentist (**match**)
17. cricket, ankle (**match**)
18. newspaper, bathe (**mismatch—bathe**)
19. England, circus (**match**)
20. veterinarian, applaud (**mismatch—applaud**)
21. stumble, friend (**mismatch—stumble**)
22. actor, computer (**match**)
23. helicopter, unbuckle (**mismatch—unbuckle**)
24. crumple, microscope (**mismatch—crumple**)
25. Eskimo, camera (**match**)

75 ADVERBS IN ACTION

Materials needed:

☐ reproducible page
☒ total group activity
☐ individual activity
☐ partner activity

TOTAL GROUP ACTIVITY

Send three students from the room. Read one of the adverbs from the following list to the class. Then have the three students return to the room. One of them calls on a classmate to act out the adverb.

The selected student first announces what he or she will be doing: eating, writing a letter, delivering mail, sorting socks, folding clothes, doing homework, and so on. For example, if the word were *lazily*, the student might lazily make a bed. Allow the student to talk as the adverb is acted out, as this generally adds to the "performance."

Each of the students who was sent from the room gets one guess as to the identity of the adverb. A synonym does not count, but if one is guessed, the "actor" should say, "Synonym," or "It means the same as the word you guessed."

If they are unsuccessful in naming the word, one of the "chosen three" selects a new student actor. Continue in this manner until each of the three players has had the opportunity to select a student actor, or until the word is guessed. Name three new students to leave the room, or have the person who guessed the word choose the new players.

Act Out These Adverbs

1. carefully
2. happily
3. quickly/hurriedly
4. slowly
5. sadly
6. carelessly
7. nervously
8. lazily
9. noisily
10. neatly
11. quietly/silently
12. carelessly
13. timidly/shyly
14. wearily
15. absent-mindedly
16. irritably
17. pleasantly
18. smugly
19. weakly
20. angrily
21. excitedly/eagerly
22. mistakenly
23. mysteriously
24. calmly
25. patiently

76 FIND ME A PARTNER

Materials needed:

☒ reproducible page
☒ total group activity
☐ individual activity
☐ partner activity

TOTAL GROUP ACTIVITY

Name a noun and ask the students to think of a variety of interesting adjectives to go with it. Encourage them to use the less commonplace adjective associations. For example, instead of "the yellow sun," they should use adjectives like "shimmering," "golden," "blazing," or "searing."

Give an Adjective to Go with ———

1.	lamb	16.	gingerbread
2.	cloud	17.	classroom
3.	boys	18.	whirlpool
4.	story	19.	ant
5.	wind	20.	metal
6.	mouse	21.	yacht
7.	kitten	22.	meadow
8.	elephant	23.	flames
9.	parrot	24.	forest
10.	car	25.	hurricane
11.	road	26.	fireworks
12.	monster	27.	greyhound
13.	river	28.	summer air
14.	chipmunk	29.	skillet
15.	light	30.	mint

REPRODUCIBLE ACTIVITY PAGE (GRADES 3–6)

Answer Key: Answers will vary.

Suggestion: If you do not have time to duplicate the reproducible page, as an alternate procedure write five to ten of the nouns from the reproducible page or Total Group Activity List on the chalkboard, and have the students write as many adjectives as possible for each.

NAME _____

FIND ME A PARTNER

Write three *interesting* adjectives to go with each
word below. Avoid words that are often overused,
like big, pretty, and nice. Instead, try to think
of words that make a vivid picture in your mind.

I'm shimmering, blazing, and searing!

1. lamb   _____ , _____ , _____

2. cloud   _____ , _____ , _____

3. boys   _____ , _____ , _____

4. wind   _____ , _____ , _____

5. kitten   _____ , _____ , _____

6. elephant   _____ , _____ , _____

7. monster   _____ , _____ , _____

8. chipmunk   _____ , _____ , _____

9. light   _____ , _____ , _____

10. ant   _____ , _____ , _____

11. meadow   _____ , _____ , _____

12. flames   _____ , _____ , _____

13. forest   _____ , _____ , _____

14. mouse   _____ , _____ , _____

15. yacht   _____ , _____ , _____

16. hurricane   _____ , _____ , _____

77   TELL ME HOW

Materials needed:

none
optional: paper and pencil for teacher

[X] reproducible page
[X] total group activity
[ ] individual activity
[ ] partner activity

TOTAL GROUP ACTIVITY

Name a verb and ask the students to think of an adverb that goes with your word. For instance, if you said "cried," they might say "hysterically."

Although there are many adverbs that can accompany each verb, ask for only one answer. Specify that adverbs may not be repeated. You, or a student recorder, could make a list of the words used, so that repetitions can be spotted easily. This activity becomes more difficult as it progresses, since the more common adverbs quickly become eliminated, and students are forced to search for other appropriate words.

Give an Adverb to Go with———

1. slept
2. dropped
3. tiptoed
4. played
5. stood
6. stopped
7. sailed
8. waved
9. touched
10. yelled
11. zigzagged
12. whispered
13. flew
14. carried
15. banged
16. disappeared
17. drove
18. wrote
19. walked
20. worked
21. paced
22. swung
23. sat
24. watched
25. danced
26. blew
27. leaned
28. maneuvered
29. cried
30. stared
31. coughed
32. floated
33. laughed
34. trudged
35. whistled

REPRODUCIBLE ACTIVITY PAGE (GRADES 4–6)

Answer Key: Answers will vary, but no words should be repeated.

NAME_____

TELL ME HOW

Read each verb below and then write an adverb that goes with the word. For instance, for the word "slept" you might write the adverb "soundly" to describe how the person slept.

Although there are many adverbs that could go with the verbs, write only one answer for each word. The tricky part about this activity is *once an adverb has been used, it cannot be repeated. Be careful!*

1. slept _____

2. dropped _____

3. tiptoed _____

4. played _____

5. stood _____

6. stopped _____

7. sailed _____

8. waved _____

9. touched _____

10. yelled _____

11. zigzagged _____

12. whispered _____

13. flew _____

14. carried _____

15. banged _____

16. disappeared _____

17. drove _____

18. wrote _____

19. walked _____

20. worked _____

21. paced _____

22. swung _____

23. sat _____

24. watched _____

25. danced _____

26. blew _____

27. leaned _____

28. laughed _____

29. cried _____

30. stared _____

31. coughed _____

32. floated _____

78   TWO-WAY WORDS

Materials needed:

☐ reproducible page
☒ total group activity
☐ individual activity
☐ partner activity

TOTAL GROUP ACTIVITY

Explain to students that the way a word is used in a sentence determines whether it is a noun, verb, adjective, or some other part of speech. From the following list read a word that can be *either* a noun or a verb. Then read the accompanying sentence. Pause to give students time to think. They should respond on the signal, "Show me," by raising their arms in the air to form a "V" if the word is a verb, or holding their arms at their sides if the word is a noun.

Variation

Materials needed:

chalkboard
chalk
eraser

Divide the class into teams and number the players. Read a word and the corresponding sentence from the list below. Player 1 on Team A must identify whether the word was used as a noun or as a verb, and use the word in its other form in a sentence. If correct, the team earns one point. If the player is incorrect, no points are earned, and Player 1 on Team B is given a chance. Alternate giving words to players on each team, keeping score on the chalkboard. When all students have had one turn, the game ends, and the team with the most points wins.

Noun or Verb?

1. COUGH: I tried not to cough during the concert. (**verb**)
2. PERMIT: I hope my dad will permit me to go to the concert. (**verb**)
3. PLAY: The school play was very funny. (**noun**)
4. DUCK: Did you see me duck when Tom threw the ball? (**verb**)
5. FACE: Please turn and face me. (**verb**)
6. STAPLE: The staple came out of the paper. (**noun**)
7. VARNISH: Dad said he is going to varnish the table today. (**verb**)
8. TIP: Mom left a tip on the table for the waitress. (**noun**)
9. PUMP: I need to buy a pump for my bicycle tires. (**noun**)
10. DIAL: As soon as Dad is off the phone, I'll dial the number. (**verb**)

11. LOOK: Dad had an angry look on his face. (**noun**)
12. ROOT: I'm going to sit here and root for our team. (**verb**)
13. ROCK: If I rock the baby, I think he will go to sleep. (**verb**)
14. DRINK: That cold drink tasted great. (**noun**)
15. LAP: I like to watch my kitten lap up its milk. (**verb**)
16. PASTE: We need some more paste. (**noun**)
17. DUST: There was dust all over the furniture. (**noun**)
18. WISH: I wish the vacation had been longer. (**verb**)
19. WAVE: The wave knocked over my sand castle. (**noun**)
20. WASH: Be certain to wash your hands before you come to dinner. (**verb**)
21. MAIL: I'll mail this letter on my way to school. (**verb**)
22. ORDER: He gave the order in a very stern voice. (**noun**)
23. CHIRP: The baby bird's chirp was shrill. (**noun**)
24. SAIL: We're hoping we can sail the boat this weekend. (**verb**)
25. DASH: I wrote a dash at the end of the word. (**noun**)
26. CRANK: They used to crank cars to get them started. (**verb**)
27. BUCKLE: The buckle fell off my new belt. (**noun**)
28. PASS: I try not to pass people without saying hello. (**verb**)
29. MIX: This is my favorite kind of cake mix. (**noun**)
30. STACK: There is a huge stack of newspapers in the garage. (**noun**)
31. DRAIN: The custodian is going to drain the water out of the sink. (**verb**)
32. CUT: Nancy had a deep cut on her leg. (**noun**)
33. HIDE: They used the animal's hide for clothing. (**noun**)
34. RATTLE: The wind made the windows rattle. (**verb**)
35. VOTE: Every vote counts in an election. (**noun**)

79 YOU ADD THE ENDING

Materials needed:

☐ reproducible page
☒ total group activity
☐ individual activity
☐ partner activity

TOTAL GROUP ACTIVITY

Before starting this activity, establish the order in which you will call on students. Read one of the following "story starters." Immediately have the first student add *one sentence* to the plot. The story line progresses from student to student with each contributing a sentence, until someone brings it to a logical conclusion. You may also intercede at an appropriate moment to suggest that an effective ending be found. Keep the pace quick and lively for full enjoyment of this activity.

Variation

An alternate method is to have a student continue telling the story, while you silently count to thirty (or whatever number you feel is appropriate). At the end of the designated time, say, "Pass," and the story progresses to the next student.

A. Who Are You? (Grades K–2)

Jamey and his big brother went fishing together at the nearby pond almost every Saturday. This particular Saturday the fishing wasn't very good, so his brother decided to try his luck on the other side of the pond. But Jamey stayed in his favorite place by the big rock. He stood there for the longest time, but there wasn't even a nibble. Everything was so quiet and still, but suddenly Jamey was startled by a tiny little voice that said, ...

B. The Sailing Adventure (Grades 1–4)

I'd always wondered about the island that had the lighthouse on it. Every night I could see the light blinking off in the distance. My parents kept saying that someday we'd sail out to the island, but we'd never done it.

Then one day during the summer, Dad said, "Let's go investigate that island you're always talking about." We put all our gear in the boat, sailed out of the harbor and under the bridge. After sailing for hours and hours, we finally neared the island. As we rounded the lighthouse, there in front of us was...

C. Bottle on the Beach (Grades 1–4)

Mike and Leslie had been at the beach all day. They'd gone swimming, built sand castles, collected shells, and dodged waves. It was almost time to leave, but they decided to walk down the beach one more time before going home.

As they walked along chatting, Mike noticed something on the sand up ahead. He was sure it hadn't been there when they walked the beach a short time ago, so he ran ahead to see what it was. When he got up close he realized it was just a bottle, but something made him stoop over and pick it up. To his surprise...

D. The Old Black Book (Grades 1–4)

Linda always loved to visit her grandmother's house. There were so many terrific things to do, but what she liked best was to go up to the attic and play.

One day when she was in the attic, she noticed an old book in the far corner. The book was covered with dust, and when Linda picked it up she could tell it was very, very old. She carefully opened it and began reading. As she read, her eyes got bigger and bigger as she realized the book told about all kinds of...

E. A Surprise Visitor (Grades 2–6)

When I got home from school my mom said she was just leaving to do the weekly grocery shopping and run some errands. She asked if I would like to come along, but I said I'd rather stay home and play my new computer game.

As soon as she left, I put my school books away and got out the game paddles. Just as I was putting the disk in the computer, I heard the doorbell ring. When I opened the door my mouth fell open in amazement. There standing in front of me was...

F. Lost in the Woods (Grades 2-6)

My parents and I had been camping and hiking in the MacDowell Wilderness area for a week and a half. I loved to camp and was sorry that we would have to go home in another few days. One afternoon, while my parents were busy around the campsite, I decided to take a short walk. I started off on the trail that was near the campsite, but before long I saw a little path that branched off to the right. Out of curiosity, I decided to follow it. After hiking awhile I decided I'd better go back so my parents wouldn't be worried. I turned around and started down the trail, taking the various branches that pointed toward the campsite. However, after walking quite awhile, I suddenly realized that nothing looked familiar. I felt a terrible sinking feeling in my stomach as I realized I was lost. I decided the best thing to do would be to...

G. New School (Grades 2–6)

David had looked forward to going to a new school, but now that he'd been there for a month, he wished with all his heart that he was still at his old school.

There wasn't really anything wrong with the new school. It was just that he didn't have any friends. As he sat at the edge of the playground watching the other students play, he started thinking about...

H. The Untraveled Country Road (Grades 4–6)

One Saturday morning I got on my bicycle and started pedaling out toward a country road I had heard about. Before long the countryside changed, and the road became quite winding and hilly, but I kept on pedaling.

I hadn't seen a car for at least an hour, and I was thinking about how nice it was to have the whole road to myself. Then suddenly...

I. Tale of the Deep Mine Shaft (Grades 4–6)

Some of my friends had told me about an old mine shaft about three miles from my house. They said that sometimes eerie sounds could be heard coming from it. I really didn't believe them, but I'll have to admit I was curious. So, one day I decided I'd go investigate.

I stood outside and listened for a while. But there wasn't a thing to be heard. It was just as I thought—they were trying to scare me. I decided that while I was there, I might as well go into the shaft and see what it was like. I took a big, heavy-duty flashlight out of my backpack, squeezed through the entrance and started to carefully climb down. Everything was going along fine until I reached about the 100-foot level. Then...

80   PARTNER RHYME CHALLENGE

Materials needed:

lined paper
pencils

☐ reproducible page
☐ total group activity
☐ individual activity
☒ partner activity

PARTNER ACTIVITY

Partners draw a line down the center of a piece of paper and choose one of the words from the following list. The word is written at the top of the paper along with their names.

They alternate saying rhyming words. Although the words must rhyme, the spelling patterns may be different, for example, *bought* and *taught*. As a word is said, the first letter or initial blend is written below the person's name. This eliminates disputes about whether or not a specific word has been said. Specify that when a letter is written, it covers all spellings of that particular word. For instance, if the initial word were *hum*, the letter "S" would represent both *sum* and *some*.

The student who names the last word receives one point. The first player with three points is the winner.

Words to Rhyme

cat	rug
hill	tail
win	wink
lap	late
hall	hop
crow	down
red	lip
ride	play
light	thumb
bake	seed

---

81 LOOK ALIKES

Materials needed:

6″ x 9″ paper
pencils
optional: crayons

☐ reproducible page
☐ total group activity
☒ individual activity
☐ partner activity

INDIVIDUAL ACTIVITY

Students write words in a way that illustrates their meaning.

These make an interesting bulletin board or can be assembled into an amusing class booklet.

82 WORD CONNECTIONS

Materials needed:

6″ x 9″ paper
pencils

☒ reproducible page
☐ total group activity
☒ individual activity
☐ partner activity

INDIVIDUAL ACTIVITY

This activity provides practice in spelling and problem solving.

Challenge students to make interlocking puzzles that connect words. By using a variety of puzzle formats, the level of difficulty can easily be adjusted.

As a supreme challenge, have students try to design a four-square by four-square interlocking puzzle, in which the words are read from right to left and from top to bottom. This activity requires much patience, but what a triumph when the puzzle finally fits together!

REPRODUCIBLE ACTIVITY PAGE (GRADES 4–6)

Answer Key: Answers will vary.

WORD CONNECTIONS

Fill in the following puzzles with words that connect. As
you try different words, write lightly so the letters can
be easily erased. When you finish a puzzle, trace over
each letter so the puzzle will be easy to read.

S	L	E	E	P
E		A		E
E		R		A
D	I	N	E	R

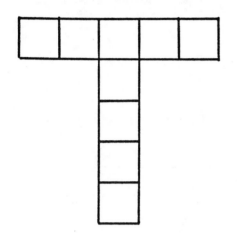

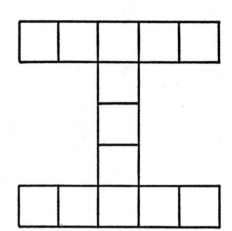

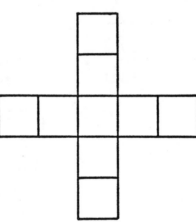

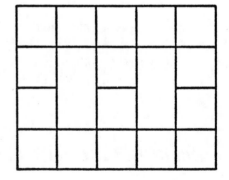

83 DOUBLE CONSONANT DAZE

Materials needed:

lined paper
pencils
dictionary

☒ reproducible page
☐ total group activity
☐ individual activity
☒ partner activity

PARTNER ACTIVITY

Partners decide on a time limit and write as many words as possible that have a *minimum of five letters* and contain a double consonant. For example: llama, giraffe, recess.

At the end of the designated time the students check each other's papers. A dictionary is used to check the spelling of disputed words. The student with the most correctly spelled words is the winner.

REPRODUCIBLE ACTIVITY PAGE (GRADES 2–6)

Have dictionaries available for students to use as they work on this activity page.

Answer Key: Answers will vary.

DOUBLE CONSONANT DAZE

How many words can you think of that have two matching consonants next to each other? Are the double consonants at the beginning, in the middle, or at the end of the word?

Write your words in the charts below. Underline the double consonants in each word.

Did you know that we have a double letter in our name?

©1989 by The Center for Applied Research in Education

Double consonants at the *beginning* of the word	Double consonants in the *middle* of the word	Double consonants at the *end* of the word
1.	1.	1.
2.	2.	2.
3.	3.	3.
4.	4.	4.
5.	5.	5.
6.	6.	6.
7.	7.	7.
8.	8.	8.
9.	9.	9.
10.	10.	10.
11.	11.	11.
12.	12.	12.

84 WORD CATEGORY EXPANSION

Materials needed:

lined paper for each person
pencils
dictionary

☒ reproducible page
☐ total group activity
☐ individual activity
☒ partner activity

PARTNER ACTIVITY

This activity provides practice in spelling and creative thinking.

Partners decide on a time limit. One of the players selects a category from the list below. The other player names a word with a minimum of six letters that belongs in the specified category. Both players write the word vertically in the left-hand margin of their papers, *skipping two lines* between each letter.

During the allotted time, the students write as many words as possible that fit in the designated category and begin with each of the letters in the vertical word. For example:

```
══════ Animals ══════
a — ant
n — newt
t — tiger
e — elephant, eagle
l — lion, leopard
o — octopus, orangutan
p — parrot
e — _____
```

When the time limit has expired, the players use a dictionary to check the spelling of any disputed words. One point is awarded for each correctly spelled word. Or, to encourage the use of longer words, students receive one point for each *letter* in words that are correctly spelled. The player with the most points is the winner.

Word Categories

animals
fruits and vegetables
girls' names
boys' names

nouns
verbs
adjectives
adverbs

things that make sounds	cities
colors	states
what you can see in the classroom	countries
items in a house	musical instruments
kitchen items	rivers
ways to get from one place to another	mountains
types of jobs	

REPRODUCIBLE ACTIVITY PAGE (GRADES 4–6)

Answer Key: Answers will vary.

WORD CATEGORY EXPANSION

Read the category at the top of each box. Then read the word written vertically along the left-hand side of the box. Write as many words as possible that belong in the category and start with the letters in the vertical word.

≣≣≣≣ Sounds ≣≣≣≣
c – creak, crunch, crash
r – roar, ruff
e – eek
a – ah
k – _____

©1989 by The Center for Applied Research in Education

ANIMALS

a _____
_____
n _____
_____
t _____
_____
e _____
_____
l _____
_____
o _____
_____
p _____
_____
e _____
_____

NOUNS

a _____
_____
i _____
_____
r _____
_____
p _____
_____
l _____
_____
a _____
_____
n _____
_____
e _____
_____

85 CATEGORIES WITH ONE-LETTER RESTRICTION

Materials needed:

lined paper for each student
pencils
dictionary

☒ reproducible page
☐ total group activity
☐ individual activity
☒ partner activity

PARTNER ACTIVITY

This activity provides practice in spelling and creative thinking.

Partners select ten categories from the list below. The students write the categories vertically down the left-hand side of the paper, skipping a line between each. Then they choose a letter of the alphabet, which is written at the top of the paper. At this point the partners may decide to work together in trying to solve the puzzle or they may compete against each other using the following format.

The partners decide on a time limit. Then each player tries to think of a word containing *five or more letters* for each category that begins with the specified letter.

When one of the students completes the entire page, or when the time limit has expired, a dictionary is used to check spelling. One point is awarded for each correctly spelled word. Or, to encourage longer words one point is earned for each *letter* in words that are correctly spelled. The player with the most points is the winner.

Categories

zoo animal	way to get from one place to another
fruit	type of job
vegetable	noun
girl's name	verb
boy's name	adjective
item that makes a sound	adverb
color	city
farm animal	state
what you can see in the classroom	country
item in a house	musical instrument
kitchen item	river
insect	mountain

REPRODUCIBLE ACTIVITY PAGE (GRADES 3–6)

This activity page may be used over and over by encouraging students to select a different letter of the alphabet each time they use the page.

Answer Key: Answers will vary.

CATEGORIES WITH ONE-LETTER RESTRICTION

Choose a letter of the alphabet and write it in the box.

Write words that belong in the categories listed below. Each word must have *at least five letters* and must start with the letter in the box.

Z	
zoo animals	zebra
vegetables	zucchini
plants	zinnia
boys' names	Zachary
girls' names	Zoe, Zona
things you could find in a house	zircon, zither
cities	Zurich

©1989 by The Center for Applied Research in Education

Write a letter of the alphabet in the box.	☐
zoo animals	
vegetables	
plants	
boys' names	
girls' names	
things you could find in the house	
cities	
states	
countries	
rivers	
things that make sound	

86 FRONT AND BACK CATEGORIES

Materials needed:

lined paper
pencils
dictionary

☒ reproducible page
☐ total group activity
☒ individual activity
☒ partner activity

INDIVIDUAL ACTIVITY

This activity provides practice in spelling and creative thinking.

Have the student divide a paper into six columns. Assign five or more categories from the list below. These are to be listed in the left-hand column. (Initially select easier topics to help build the student's confidence and sense of success, then assign the more challenging topics.)

In the second column, one word is written that belongs in each of the specified categories. "Category words" in the third through sixth columns must begin with the *last letter* of the preceding word. Students fill in as many sections of the puzzle grid as they can.

cities	Detroit	Toledo	Oakland	Dallas	Seattle
ways to move from one place to another	airplane	elevator			
girls' names					
boys' names					

PARTNER ADAPTATION (GRADES 3–6)

Partners divide their paper into six columns and alternate naming six categories, which are recorded in the left-hand column.

At this point the partners decide whether they would prefer working together to try to solve the puzzle or whether they would rather compete against each other. They then try to fill in as many spaces on the grid as possible. Each word must begin with the last letter of the preceding word and must belong in the designated category. A dictionary is used to check spelling.

If they are competing against one another, one point is awarded for each correctly spelled word. The student with the most points is the winner.

Front and Back Categories

animals	ways to get from one place to another
fruits and vegetables	types of jobs
girls' names	nouns
boys' names	verbs
colors	adjectives
things that make sounds	adverbs
items in a house	cities
what you can see it the classroom	states

REPRODUCIBLE ACTIVITY PAGE (GRADES 3–6)

Answer Key: Answers will vary.

NAME _____

FRONT AND BACK CATEGORIES

Read the categories listed in the left-hand column below. In the second column, write a word that fits in each of the categories.

For the next column, try to think of a new word for each category that *begins with the last letter of the preceding word.* The first few words have been written for you. Fill in as many sections of the puzzle as you can.

	dog	→ giraffe →	e						
animals									
items found in a house									
plants									
things in the classroom									
girls' names									
boys' names									
fruits and vegetables									
colors									
things that make sounds									
states									

87   ONE-LETTER MAGIC

Materials needed:

lined paper
pencils

☒ reproducible page
☐ total group activity
☒ individual activity
☐ partner activity

INDIVIDUAL ACTIVITY

This activity provides spelling practice, builds vocabulary, and develops creative thinking.

Students make a list of words that can be made into new words by the addition of one letter. The letters of the initial word must remain in the same order, but the new letter may be placed at the beginning or end of the word, or inserted between any of the letters. Neither an "S" nor an "E" may be added at the end of a word.

Examples:

1. lead——plead
2. fist——first
3. bead——bread
4. power——powder
5. pant——paint

Older students can extend the activity to make a puzzle challenge for other students. In this case, each word pair is numbered to form an answer sheet. The paper is turned over and a clue is written for each of the words. For example:

Add one letter to lead and you'll have a word that tells what you do if you beg for something.

REPRODUCIBLE ACTIVITY PAGE (GRADES 3–6)

Answer Key: Answers will vary. Possible answers follow. (1) starts, (2) powder, (3) world, (4) chop, (5) black, (6) spin, (7) beard, (8) chill, (9) when, (10) plead, (11) pound, (12) first, (13) weed, (14) four, (15) bread, (16) paint, (17) pearl, (18) trips, (19) barns, (20) brat, (21) plant, (22) spell, (23) house, (24) smile, (25) tiny, (26) raft, (27) chief, (28) cheap.

NAME _____

ONE-LETTER MAGIC

Add *one* letter to each of the following words to make a new word. The letter may be added at the beginning, the end, or anywhere within the word. Neither an *s* nor an *e* may be added at the end of a word, and each of the new words must be different.

ADD ONE LETTER TO MAKE A NEW WORD		ADD ONE LETTER TO MAKE A NEW WORD	
1. stars	starts	15. bead	
2. power		16. pant	
3. word		17. pear	
4. hop		18. tips	
5. back		19. bars	
6. pin		20. bat	
7. bear		21. plan	
8. hill		22. sell	
9. hen		23. hose	
10. lead		24. mile	
11. pond		25. tin	
12. fist		26. rat	
13. wed		27. chef	
14. for		28. heap	

88   TIC-TAC-TOE SPELLING

Materials needed:

lined paper

pencils

dictionary

☐ reproducible page
☐ total group activity
☐ individual activity
☒ partner activity

PARTNER ACTIVITY

This activity provides practice in spelling and creative thinking.

A grid of seven lines down and seven lines across is drawn on a piece of paper. Players attempt to complete words that are three or more letters in length.

The first player prints a letter in one of the squares. The other player must print a letter in a square that has a common side (above, below, or to either side). The letter may not be written in a diagonal square.

Players continue taking turns writing letters until no new words can be formed. When a word is completed, a line is drawn through it, and the player receives one point for each letter in the word. The same player then writes one new letter to continue the game. Points are awarded if a player adds a letter to a word to form a new word. Therefore if four points had been scored for the word *plan*, the other player could add a "t" and receive five points for the word *plant*. Changing words from singular to plural is not allowed. Students should use a dictionary if the spelling of a word is questioned.

If a player cannot complete a word, a letter must be written that helps form a longer word which will fit within the grid. If the opponent feels the letter is not part of a real word, the player says, "I challenge." If the player was bluffing or the intended word is misspelled, the challenger gets five points; however if the player names an appropriate word, he or she immediately gets to complete the word, filling in the necessary squares. One point is awarded for each letter in the word. If a player says no additional words can be written within the grid, and the opponent is able to think of a word that will fit, he or she may fill in the entire word and receive one point for each letter.

89   GROWING WORD BOXES

Materials needed:

lined paper for each student
pencils
dictionary

☒ reproducible page
☐ total group activity
☐ individual activity
☒ partner activity

PARTNER ACTIVITY

This activity gives spelling practice and builds vocabulary.

Partners select a word with four to six letters in which no letters are repeated. The left-hand edge of the paper is numbered 3 through 8. For younger students you may wish to make the highest number 5 or 6; with upper-grade students, the numbering can extend beyond 8. The remainder of the paper is ruled into as many columns as there are letters in the chosen word. The letters of the word are written at the top of the columns.

	d	e	s	k
3	did	eat		
4	done	even		
5	daisy			
6	dinner			
7	delight			
8	delicate			

Beginning with the first letter of their word ("d" in the example here), they write a three-letter word that begins with that letter, a four-letter word beginning with the same letter on the next line, then a five-letter word, and so on. The same procedure is followed for each of the other letters in the selected word. Root words cannot appear more than once, for example strange, strangest. Plurals, proper names, and foreign words are not allowed.

The students may choose to work together in solving the puzzle, or they may compete against one another using the following format.

The partners decide how much time will be spent developing their word lists. The challenge is to see who can write the most correctly spelled words within the allotted time. At the end of the time period, partners exchange papers and use a dictionary to check spelling. One point is awarded for each correctly spelled word. The person with the most points is the winner.

Variation

After students have worked many "Growing Word Boxes," they find that the vowels are repeated over and over. For instance, if they chose the words *desk*, *life*, and *pencil*, they would discover that "e" appeared in each of these words. This eliminates some of the challenge of working the puzzle. For variety, have them select single letters at random and build "staircases" of words that begin with the selected letter.

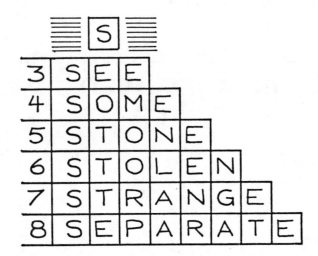

REPRODUCIBLE ACTIVITY PAGES (GRADES 3–6)

There are two different reproducible pages that accompany this activity.

Answer Key: Answers will vary.

NAME _____

©1989 by The Center for Applied Research in Education

GROWING WORD BOXES

Read the word at the top of the puzzle. Begin with the first letter of the word, *t*. In the first space, write a three-letter word that begins with *t*. In the next space, write a four-letter word that begins with the same letter, then a five-letter word, and so on. Fill in as many boxes as possible.

Do the same thing with the other letters in the word.

	t	r	i	c	k	e	d	
3								
4								
5								
6								
7								
8								
9								

	m	a	n
3	mad	ate	nod
4	made	able	noon
5	meaty	after	never
6	mother	always	number
7	mention	another	nothing

MORE GROWING WORD BOXES

Write a letter in one of the circles. In the first row, write a three-letter word that begins with the letter in the circle. In the next row write a four-letter word that begins with the same letter, then a five-letter word, and so on.

Do the same thing with all of the puzzles, except a *different* letter must be written in each circle.

3	j	o	y		
4	j	o	i	n	
5	j	u	i	c	y
6	j	u	m	p	e	d
7	j	i	n	g	l	e	s
8	j	u	g	g	l	i	n	g

90 ROVING LETTERS

Materials needed:

6″ x 9″ paper
pencils
optional: dictionary

☒ reproducible page
☐ total group activity
☒ individual activity
☒ partner activity

INDIVIDUAL ACTIVITY

These student-made puzzles can become challenges for fellow classmates.

To make a Roving Letter Puzzle, the student draws a nine-square grid and then thinks of (or looks in a dictionary to find) a nine-letter word. Each letter of the word is written sequentially diagonally, above, below, or to either side of the preceding letter. The word is also written on the reverse side of the paper, to serve as an answer sheet.

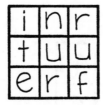 

When you have collected a sufficient number of these puzzles, assemble them into a word puzzle book for the enjoyment of the class.

PARTNER ADAPTATION (GRADES 4–6)

Both students write a nine-letter word within a nine-square grid, so that each letter is written sequentially diagonally, above, below, or to the side of the preceding letter.

Partners exchange papers. The first one to discover the other person's word receives one point. The process is repeated, using new words. The first person with five points is the winner.

REPRODUCIBLE ACTIVITY PAGE (GRADES 4–6)

Answer Key: (1) discovery, (2) magazines, (3) scientist, (4) parachute, (5) equipment, (6) listening, (7) curiosity, (8) fantastic, (9) thousands.

ROVING LETTERS

A word is hidden in each of the the squares below. The letters in the word are connected in order: above, below, to either side, or diagonally.

When you find the word, put a dot by the first letter, then draw a line, connecting the letters in order. Put an "x" by the last letter. Write the word on the line below the box.

i	n	r
t	u	u
e	r	f

__furniture__

1.
y	r	e
i	s	v
d	c	o

_____

2.
s	a	g
e	z	a
n	i	m

_____

3.
t	c	i
s	s	e
i	t	n

_____

4.
p	c	h
a	a	u
r	e	t

_____

5.
i	u	q
p	m	e
t	n	e

_____

6.
g	n	i
i	s	n
l	t	e

_____

7.
y	t	u
i	c	r
s	o	i

_____

8.
n	t	a
f	a	s
c	i	t

_____

9.
n	s	u
d	a	o
s	t	h

_____

91   ANAGRAMS

Materials needed:

6″ x 9″ paper
pencil

☒ reproducible page
☐ total group activity
☒ individual activity
☐ partner activity

INDIVIDUAL ACTIVITY

This activity provides practice in spelling and creative thinking.

Anagrams are words whose letters can be rearranged to make one or more new words. For example, four anagrams can be formed from the word *stop*: post, pots, tops, spot.

On one side of a piece of 6″ x 9″ paper the students should write a word and indicate how many words can be made by rearranging the letters. The answer(s) are written on the back of the paper.

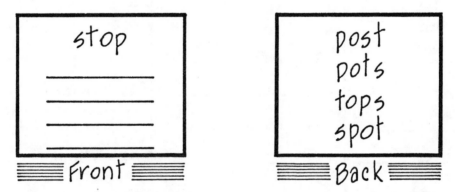

The completed papers can be placed in a designated area as challenges for other students.

REPRODUCIBLE ACTIVITY PAGE (GRADES 4–6)

Answer Key: (1) horse, (2) read, dear; (3) words; (4) east, eats, seat; (5) never; (6) bowl; (7) peach; (8) meat, tame, team; (9) taste; (10) wasp; (11) plate, petal; (12) plum; (13) north; (14) scalp; (15) care, race; (16) snap, pans, naps; (17) lamp; (18) limes, miles, smile; (19) tales, stale, steal, least.

ANAGRAMS

Anagrams are words whose letters can be rearranged to make one or more new words. For example four anagrams can be made from the word *stop*: post, pots, tops, spot.

Write anagrams for the following words.

1. shore

   _____

2. dare

   _____

   _____

3. sword

   _____

4. teas

   _____

   _____

   _____

5. nerve

   _____

6. blow

   _____

7. cheap

   _____

8. mate

   _____

   _____

   _____

9. state

   _____

10. paws

    _____

11. pleat

    _____

    _____

12. lump

    _____

13. thorn

    _____

14. clasp

    _____

15. acre

    _____

    _____

16. span

    _____

    _____

    _____

17. palm

    _____

18. slime

    _____

    _____

    _____

19. slate

    _____

    _____

    _____

    _____

92   WORD SUBTRACTION

Materials needed:

6″ x 9″ paper
pencils

☐ reproducible page
☐ total group activity
☒ individual activity
☐ partner activity

INDIVIDUAL ACTIVITY

The student selects two words. The letters of the words are scrambled, but the order of letters within *each word* is maintained.

giraffe pencil ≡ gpireafncifle

The jumbled word with some spaces inserted, is written on one side of a piece of 6″ x 9″ paper. The student writes clues about the identity of the two words. The answer is written on the reverse side of the paper.

gpire afnc ifle
Take away an animal
and something you
write with will be left.

≡ Front ≡

Take away giraffe.

Answer: pencil.

≡ Back ≡

When you have collected a sufficient number of these, assemble them into a word puzzle book for the class to enjoy.

93   SCRAMBLED SENTENCES

Materials needed:

6″ x 9″ paper
pencils

☐ reproducible page
☐ total group activity
☒ individual activity
☒ partner activity

INDIVIDUAL ACTIVITY

The student writes a sentence on one side of the paper. This becomes the answer sheet. (You may want to specify that the sentence must relate to a current unit of study or a specific subject.) On the reverse side of the paper the sentence is written so that the letters within each word are "scrambled," but the order of words remains the same.

As these are completed, have them put in a designated place to be used as challenges for the other students.

reeTh era nnei sepatln ni hte lorsa tssyme.

≡ Front ≡

There are nine planets in the solar system.

≡ Back ≡

PARTNER ADAPTATION (GRADES 4–6)

Materials needed:

lined paper
pencils

Partners agree on the number of words they will write in a sentence. They each write a sentence on one side of a piece of paper. This becomes their answer sheet.

The same sentence is copied over with the sequence of letters in each word scrambled. Students fold the answer section under, and exchange papers. The first person to decode the partner's sentence receives one point. New sentences are written and the process repeated until one student has three points.

94 CAN YOU FOLLOW MY DIRECTIONS?

Materials needed:

☒ reproducible page
☒ total group activity
☐ individual activity
☐ partner activity

TOTAL GROUP ACTIVITY

Students sit on their chairs, which have been moved about an arm's length in back of their desks. Remaining seated with eyes closed, they follow the series of directions below, for example, "Fold arms, turn head to right, touch pointing fingers." The final instruction is, "Freeze. You should be in this position." Slowly read the position to the children and have them check to see if they are in the position you describe.

Variation

Rather than using the entire series of directions with younger students, you may want to stop half way through. For this reason, a description of the students' position is given after the tenth instruction. (If your students enjoyed this activity, "Close Your Eyes" and "Put Your Hands on Your Knees" are similar exercises in following a series of directions.)

Oral Directions

1. Close your eyes and remain seated.
2. Fold your arms.
3. Turn your head to the right.
4. Shrug your shoulders five times.
5. Make your pointing fingers touch.
6. Flap your elbows three times.
7. Stretch your feet out in front of you.
8. Wiggle your feet.
9. Put both hands behind your neck.
10. Put your right hand on your left elbow.
    (If you stop at this point, say, "Freeze. You should be in this position.")
    POSITION: Sitting, eyes closed, feet stretched out in front, left hand behind neck, right hand on left elbow, and head turned to the right.
11. Put your right hand between your shoulder blades.
12. Place your right foot flat on the floor.
13. Grab your right ear with your left hand.

14. Rest your head on your left shoulder.
15. Lean to the left.
    POSITION: Sitting, eyes closed, left foot stretched out in front, right foot flat on floor, left hand grabbing right ear, right hand between shoulder blades, head resting on left shoulder, and body leaning to the left.

REPRODUCIBLE ACTIVITY PAGE (GRADES 3–6)

If there is time after the students have completed the reproducible page, have them discuss what happened when they read their directions to someone else. Elicit ways they could make their directions easier to understand. After this discussion you may want to repeat the activity, having the students apply what they learned.

Answer Key: Answers will vary.

CAN YOU FOLLOW MY DIRECTIONS?

...are you SURE this is what I'm supposed to do?

Write a series of ten directions that a person could do while seated. For example: (1) fold your hands, (2) cross your feet, and so on.

After you have written all ten directions, follow your own directions. Then write what the final position should be. Follow the directions several more times to make certain the description of the final position is correct.

Now read your directions to someone and see what happens!

1. _____

2. _____

3. _____

4. _____

5. _____

6. _____

7. _____

8. _____

9. _____

10. _____

| FINAL POSITION | _____ |

_____

_____

| WHAT HAPPENED WHEN YOU READ THE DIRECTIONS TO SOMEONE ELSE? |

_____

_____

_____

95   CLOSE YOUR EYES

Materials needed:

TOTAL GROUP ACTIVITY

The students follow a series of directions while seated in chairs with their eyes closed (for example, "Face the sink, stretch arms to either side, put left hand on left ankle," etc.). The final instruction is, "Freeze. You should be in this position." Slowly read the position to the children and have them check to see if they are in the position you describe.

Variation

Rather than using the entire series of directions, with younger students you may want to stop after ten directions. For this reason, a description of the students' position is given after the tenth instruction.

Oral Directions

1. Face the sink.
2. Close your eyes.
3. Stretch your arms out to the side.
4. Put your left hand on your left ankle.
5. Turn your body so it is facing me.
6. Put your right hand on your back.
7. Twist your body back and forth three times.
8. Stretch up both hands over your head.
9. Put your right foot on top of your left foot.
10. Put your left hand on your chest.
    (If you stop at this point, say, "Freeze. You should be in this position.")
    POSITION: Sitting, eyes closed, right hand stretched up over head, left hand on chest, and right foot on top of left foot.
11. Put your right hand on your left knee.
12. Tilt your face toward the ceiling.
13. Put your right hand on your chin.
14. Keep your hands where they are and make your thumbs touch.
    POSITION: Sitting, eyes closed, head tilted toward ceiling, left hand on chest, right hand on chin, and thumbs touching.

96   PUT YOUR HANDS ON YOUR KNEES

Materials needed:

☐ reproducible page
☒ total group activity
☐ individual activity
☐ partner activity

TOTAL GROUP ACTIVITY

The students follow a series of directions while seated in chairs with their eyes closed (for example, "Tilt head toward ceiling, put right hand on head, tuck in lips," etc.) The final instruction is, "Freeze. You should be in this position." Slowly read the position to the children and have them check to see if they are in the position you describe.

Variation

Rather than using the entire series of directions with younger students, you may want to stop after ten directions. For this reason, a description of the students' position is given after the tenth instruction.

Oral Directions

1. Put your hands on your knees.
2. Close your eyes.
3. Stick your elbows out.
4. Nod your head three times.
5. Put your right hand on your head.
6. Tuck your lips in.
7. Put your left hand on your nose.
8. Jiggle your feet.
9. Bend over.
10. Sit tall.

    (If you stop at this point, say, "Freeze. You should be in this position.")
    (POSITION: Eyes closed, right hand on head, left hand on nose, sitting tall with lips tucked in.)

11. Put your right hand behind your right knee.
12. Reach behind your knees and grab your right hand with your left hand.
13. Smile.
14. Put your left foot behind your right ankle.
15. Tilt your body to the right.

    (POSITION: Eyes closed, right hand and left hand grasped behind right knee, left foot behind right ankle, body tilted to right, smiling!)

97 MYSTERY SENTENCE MAGIC

Materials needed:
½ sheet of paper for each student
pencils

☐ reproducible page
☒ total group activity
☐ individual activity
☐ partner activity

TOTAL GROUP ACTIVITY

Have the students write the following words on their papers.

> LIMPING HOPE HITS HOT FUNNY WITHIN THAT OPEN

Then tell them to follow the directions you read from the list below. If everything is done correctly, they will have a humorous message on their paper when they are finished.

Oral Directions

1. In the first word, change *LI* to *JU*.
2. Change *H* to *R* in the second word.
3. Cross off the *H* and *T* in the third word.
4. Change *H* to *N* in the fourth word.
5. Cross off the last two letters in the fifth word.
6. Change *IN* to *OUT* in the sixth word.
7. Cross off the first two letters and the last letter in the seventh word.
8. Put an *R* at the beginning of the last word, and cross off the last letter.

Answer Key:

> JU   R   N   OUT   R
> L͟I͟MPING H͟OPE H͟IT͟S H͟OT FUNN͟Y͟ WITH͟I͟N͟ T͟H͟AT͟ OPEN͟
> (Jumping rope is not fun without a rope!)

98 LETTER MAZE

Materials needed:

unlined paper
pencils

☐ reproducible page
☒ total group activity
☐ individual activity
☐ partner activity

TOTAL GROUP ACTIVITY

Read the following directions to the students and have them follow them on unlined paper. Tell them that they may write either upper case or lower case letters for this activity.

Letter Maze Directions

1. Write the letter *G* in the middle of your paper.
2. In the bottom right-hand corner write an exclamation point.
3. To the left of the *G*, at the left-hand edge of the paper, write the letter *F*.
4. To the right of the *G*, at the right-hand edge of the paper, write a *T*.
5. In the bottom left-hand corner, write the letter *B*.
6. Above the *T*, at the top of the page, write *H*.
7. In the upper left-hand corner, write *I*.
8. Halfway between the *I* and the *H*, write *E*.
9. At the bottom of the page, below the *G*, write *R*.
10. Say the vowels to yourself. Cross out the second vowel with an *X*.
11. Connect the *T* and the exclamation point with a dotted line.
12. Cross out the second letter of the alphabet with an *X*.
13. Draw a straight line between the letters *H* and *T*.
14. Make a box around the letter *F*, and color it in.
15. Draw a line from *I* to *G* to *H*.
16. Draw a straight line from *R* to *I*.
17. If you have followed the directions correctly, the letters that are connected by the straight lines spell a word. What word do they spell? (Right!)

Answer Key:

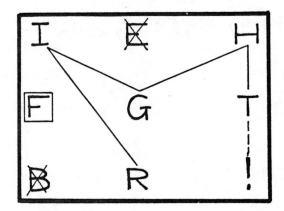

99   TWO BOX TEASER

Materials needed:

unlined paper
pencils

☐ reproducible page
☒ total group activity
☐ individual activity
☐ partner activity

TOTAL GROUP ACTIVITY

Draw the following diagrams on the chalkboard and have the students copy them on paper. Then read the following set of directions and have the students follow them. An answer key is provided below.

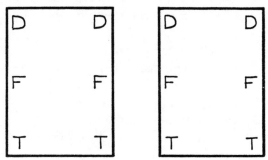

Two Box Teaser Directions

1. In the right-hand box, find the *F* in the right-hand column. Draw a square around it.
2. In the right-hand box, find the *T* in the right-hand column. Draw an *X* on it.
3. In the left-hand box, find the *D* in the upper left-hand corner. Put a square around it.
4. In the right-hand box, find the *D* in the upper left-hand corner. Draw a circle around it.
5. In the left-hand box, find the *F* in the right-hand column. Put an *X* on it.
6. In the left-hand box, find the *T* in the bottom left-hand column. Draw a circle around it.
7. In the right-hand box, find the *F* in the left-hand column. Put a check on it.
8. In the left-hand box, find the *D* in the upper right-hand column. Put a check on it.

Answer Key:

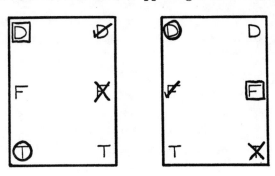

100   REPEAT THESE NUMBERS

Materials needed:

lined paper
pencils

☐ reproducible page
☒ total group activity
☐ individual activity
☐ partner activity

TOTAL GROUP ACTIVITY

Have the students hold their pencils in the air while you read a number series from the following list. At first read only the first four or five numbers in the series. Gradually increase the length of the series as students get better at the activity. As soon as you say the last number, raise your hand in the air. At this signal, the students should try to write the numbers in the same order, then raise their pencils in the air once more.

Students should keep their pencils in the air while you repeat the number sequence and they visually check their answer. Then have them mark their answers. Repeat the same procedure with a new number.

If you find students who are especially good at this activity, ask if they have any special techniques that help them. This can evolve into an interesting class discussion about ways of learning and remembering. Make certain students understand that different people learn in different ways, and that it is important for them to discover the techniques that work best for *them*.

How Many Numbers Can You Repeat?

1.	3, 6, 8, 4, 2, 9, 1, 7, 5	11.	6, 8, 3, 9, 1, 4, 7, 2, 5
2.	5, 7, 2, 9, 4, 1, 2, 6, 8	12.	7, 2, 8, 3, 9, 1, 5, 7, 4
3.	8, 2, 9, 4, 3, 7, 5, 1, 7	13.	8, 5, 9, 1, 4, 2, 7, 3, 6
4.	4, 7, 2, 9, 7, 1, 5, 3, 8	14.	1, 5, 7, 6, 2, 8, 3, 4, 9
5.	2, 7, 4, 9, 1, 5, 8, 3, 4	15.	5, 7, 9, 1, 6, 2, 7, 4, 3
6.	7, 3, 8, 2, 9, 1, 3, 6, 7	16.	3, 5, 1, 7, 2, 8, 4, 9, 5
7.	6, 2, 9, 5, 8, 4, 2, 7, 1	17.	4, 8, 1, 9, 7, 2, 8, 3, 6
8.	9, 7, 4, 6, 1, 3, 8, 2, 5	18.	2, 6, 9, 7, 1, 8, 4, 6, 3
9.	1, 8, 3, 9, 2, 1, 7, 3, 4	19.	9, 3, 7, 4, 5, 8, 2, 9, 1
10.	4, 7, 2, 9, 1, 6, 5, 4, 8	20.	5, 8, 3, 9, 2, 6, 1, 7, 2

101　EXPANDING SENTENCES

Materials needed:

☐ reproducible page
☒ total group activity
☐ individual activity
☐ partner activity

TOTAL GROUP ACTIVITY

This activity is designed to challenge students' listening abilities.

Read a short sentence from the list below and have a student repeat it. Read the same sentence again, but with an addition to make it longer. Continue to add to the sentence until it has been read and repeated four different times.

You may want to select one student to repeat all of the variations of the same sentence, or you may prefer to rotate the activity among the students. The latter is especially fun if students are seated in rows or in a circle. When someone makes a mistake the same sentence "passes on" to the next person (without being read again) and continues from student to student until someone repeats it correctly. The next expanding sentence is then read and the game continues as above.

When the fourth expansion is said correctly you may want to ask if any other students would like to repeat it. After several repetitions you will find that some of the less secure students begin to volunteer. This results in keeping everyone involved in the activity and promoting a feeling of success for all.

Can You Repeat My Sentence?

1.　My dog always chews his bone.
　　My dog always chews his bone in the back yard.
　　My dog always chews his bone in the back yard, except when another dog comes along.
　　My dog always chews his bone in the back yard, except when another dog comes along and
　　　barks at him.

2.　My mother always bakes cookies.
　　My mother always bakes cookies for me to take to school in my lunch.
　　My mother always bakes cookies for me to take to school in my lunch, except when she is
　　　very busy.
　　My mother always bakes cookies for me to take to school in my lunch, except when she is
　　　very busy or when she is not feeling well.

3.　It's fun to ski down steep hills.
　　It's fun to ski down steep hills as fast as you can.
　　It's fun to ski down steep hills as fast as you can while it's snowing.
　　It's fun to ski down steep hills as fast as you can while it's snowing and the wind is blowing.

4. I saw an interesting bird.
   I saw an interesting bird with black, white, and red feathers.
   I saw an interesting bird with black, white, and red feathers perched high up in the tree.
   I saw an interesting bird with black, white, and red feathers perched high up in the tree next to my house.

5. I heard the sound of rain.
   I heard the sound of rain as it hit the roof.
   I heard the sound of rain as it hit the roof and blew against my window.
   I heard the sound of rain as it hit the roof and blew against my window all night long.

6. Last night I saw a sailboat.
   Last night I saw a sailboat with its sails raised.
   Last night I saw a sailboat with its sails raised gliding across the water.
   Last night I saw a sailboat with its sails raised gliding across the water, just as the sun began to set.

7. I saw John sitting in a chair.
   I saw John sitting in a chair reading a book.
   I saw John sitting in a chair reading a book in the library.
   I saw John sitting in a chair reading a book in the library during our first recess yesterday.

8. It's best to go to the store in the afternoon.
   It's best to go to the store in the afternoon on a Thursday.
   It's best to go to the store in the afternoon on a Thursday to do your grocery shopping.
   It's best to go to the store in the afternoon on a Thursday to do your grocery shopping, while the crowds are small.

9. I saw a dog.
   I saw a dog shaking itself.
   I saw a dog shaking itself at the edge of the water.
   I saw a dog shaking itself at the edge of the water, after it had been swimming in the lake.

10. We made a snowman.
    We made a snowman yesterday.
    We made a snowman yesterday late in the afternoon.
    We made a snowman yesterday late in the afternoon, just before we went inside to eat dinner.

102   CAN YOU ADD TO MY SENTENCE?

Materials needed:

☐ reproducible page
☒ total group activity
☐ individual activity
☐ partner activity

TOTAL GROUP ACTIVITY

Decide on the order in which students will take turns. Read one of the beginning phrases from the following list and challenge students to see how long a sentence they can build and remember! Specify that the word "and" may be used only once within any sentence.

Each student in turn repeats the sentence and adds one new word. This continues until the sentence is repeated incorrectly or the next student is unable to add a word.

Score is kept by holding up a finger as each new word is said. You may begin the next round with a different phrase or repeat the same phrase and have them build a different sentence.

Example:

As I was

As I was walking

As I was walking along

As I was walking along one

As I was walking along one Sunday

As I was walking along one Sunday afternoon,...

Sentence Starters

1. A huge lion...
2. As I was....
3. After lunch...
4. When I went...
5. On a cold day...
6. Coming home from...
7. One dark night...
8. Near the forest...

9. When I...
10. In the middle of...
11. On the way...
12. In my room...
13. When lunch is over...
14. On the street...
15. The tiny puppy...